The Résumé Reference Book

The Résumé Reference Book

by
Howard Lauther

McFarland & Company, Inc., Publishers
Jefferson, North Carolina, and London

British Library Cataloguing-in-Publication data are available

Library of Congress Cataloguing-in-Publication Data

Lauther, Howard, 1935–
    The résumé reference book / by Howard Lauther.
      p.   cm.
    Includes index.
    ISBN 0-89950-498-1 (sewn softcover: 55# alk. paper) ∞
    1. Résumés (Employment)   I. Title.
HF5383.L35   1990
650.14 — dc20   89-43711
                                                CIP

Manufactured in the United States of America

McFarland & Company, Inc., Publishers
  Box 611, Jefferson, North Carolina 28640

To my mother
Ina Lauther
the best friend
I have ever had.

Table of Contents

Introduction   1

Writing the Résumé   3
Name, Address, and Tele-
  phone Number   3
Opening Paragraph   4
  The Heading   4
  Opening Words   5
  Statement of
    Experience   6
  Knowledge Gained   6
  Types of Employers   8
  Preferences   9
Personal Profile   10
  The Heading   10
  Skills   10
  Talents   12
  Personal Sketch   13
Education   14
  The Heading   14
  Order of Importance   14
  College Degree   15
  College Major   16
  College Minor   17
  Scholarships   17
  Honors   18
  Grade Point
    Average   18
  Dean's List   19
  College Expenses   19
  Individual Courses   20

No Degree   20
Seminars   21
Company and Correspon-
  dence Courses   22
Military Education   22
High School   23
Book Reading   24
Education Intentions   25
Employment   25
  The Heading   25
  Employer's Name   26
  Job Title   26
  Salary   27
  Work Environment   27
  Job Descriptions   28
  Knowledge Gained   31
  Reason for Leaving   31
  New Graduate   31
  Career Changer   35
  Entering Civilian Life   35
  Military Rank   36
Achievements   36
  The Heading   37
  Nonachievements   37
Miscellaneous   40
  Testimonials   40
  Work Philosophy   41
  Hobbies and Interests   42
  Memberships   42
  Activities   42
  New Graduate   43
  Awards   44

Table of Contents

Personal Statistics   44
Past Military Back-
    ground   45
Publications   45
Salary Requirement   46
References   46

Editing Your Résumé   47
An Overview   47
What Are You Selling?   48
Deleting   49
Combining   49
Redundancies   50
Order of Importance   51
Added Words and
    Phrases   51
Opening Paragraph   52
Choosing the Tense   52
Definite Objective   52
Identifying a Career
    Field   53
Unclear Objective   54
Almost a Definite Objec-
    tive   55
Skills, Traits, and
    Talents   56
Education   57
No Degree   58
Abbreviations   58
Odds and Ends   58
Employment   59
Some Tips   60
Job Title   60
The Employment "Pref-
    ace"   62
Career Changer   63
New Graduate   64
Similar Jobs   64
Eliminating Em-
    ployers   64

Employment Dates   65
Contrasting Jobs   65
Achievements   66
After It's Edited   68

Layout and Design   71
The Layout   71
Design   72
The Importance of De-
    sign   72
The Typing Stage   73
Contracting for the Typing
    73
Essential Options   74
Right-Hand Justification
    75
Typestyles   75
Name & Address   76
Headings   77
Whitespace   77
Abuse of Whitespace   78
Margins   78
Spacing   78
Bullets, Asterisks, Etc.   79
Photographs   79
Other Design Tech-
    niques   80

Going to Press   81
Proofreading   81
Spelling   81
Grammar   81
Questions Before Print-
    ing   82
Length   83
Duplicating Your Ré-
    sumé   84
The Copy Machine   84
The Quick Printer   85

Table of Contents

Paper   85
Mistakes After Printing   86

Sample Résumés   87

Functional Résumé   107
The Procedure   107
Conclusion   108

Internal Promotion   111
The Procedure   111

Mailing the Résumé   115
An Advertisement   115
A Reference Guide   115
Highlighting an Item   116
Into the Envelope   117

The Interview   119
Help Wanted Ads   119
Headhunters   120
Book on Job Hunting   121
Job Search Principles   121
Before and During the Interview   122

Contacted by
    Phone   123
Bad Reference   123
Salary Discussion   123
Interview Questions   124

Letters   127
Cover Letter   127
    Three Examples   128
    Stationery   129
    Getting Names   129
The Memo   130
The Broadcast Letter   131
Letter on Behalf   133
Acceptance Letter   134
Declining an Offer   135
Resignation Letter   136
The Business Card   136
    The Contents   137

Index   139

Introduction

This is a reference book for the job hunter who wishes to do one of the following:

1. Prepare a new résumé.
2. Refer to specific information about résumé development or presentation for the purpose of correcting any errors, or improving the information regarding one that has already been written.

While it is indeed difficult to be all things to all people, this book has been written to satisfy the unique needs of four different kinds of job hunters.

The Job Changer: This individual is not usually dissatisfied with his career; he just feels he can better himself by going to work for another employer. He could be looking for more money, more challenges, a more impressive title, or whatever. He needs a résumé to sell his past experience and proven capabilities.

The Career Changer: This person does not want to continue doing the same kind of work. It may bore her, or she sees no future in it, or perhaps she has become attracted to something else. Whichever way you look at it, she is starting over. She needs a résumé that says to the employer: "I am not too old or set in my ways to change horses at midstream and do a great job for you."

The New Graduate: A job hunter in this group just wants to get her foot in the door. She is not terribly picky, as long as you point her in the right direction and pay her enough money so that she can pay off her education. She wants a résumé that reeks of potential and tickles the imagination of the employer.

1

Introduction

The Dischargee: Fresh out of the military, he can be a seeker of employment much like the new graduate; however, if he has been trained to do something he rather likes, he also has the advantage of acting like the Job Changer (described above) as well. He needs a résumé that can help him cross the bridge into civilian life.

While there are indeed some techniques which all writers of their own résumés must use to appeal to an employer's better nature (writing one's name and address is one), the other approaches can vary greatly according to the job hunter's current situation, as previously shown.

Therefore, if you are beginning your résumé "from scratch," remember that not everything in this book will apply to you. When that occurs, skip over it and continue on. (Some information, for example, pertains only to the job changer, or the career changer, or the new graduate, or the person getting out of the military.)

Finally, if you are using this reference book on résumé writing to simply see how you might improve what you *already* have, include what you *don't* have, or omit what you should *not* have. Remember that the suggestions offered may differ greatly from you have been told by someone else or from what you have read in another book on the same subject. When that occurs you are on your own, and you will have to decide whose advice to follow — theirs or mine.

Howard Lauther

Writing the Résumé

Name, Address, and Telephone Number

Save your formality for the application form. If you like Tom instead of Thomas, then use it. Furthermore if everyone calls you by your nickname, and that nickname isn't funny-sounding, you may use it in place of your first and middle name. For example, if someone calls your home and asks for Anthony instead of Tony, the person answering may be caught off guard—perhaps even saying that no one is there by that name before they realize their error.

If you are known by your middle name, use it. Write your first name as an initial. A nickname may be used as long as it is as common as most first names. Do not use Mr., Ms., or Mrs.; avoid putting Jr. after your name, unless there's a likelihood they will confuse you with your father.

> Henry L. Townsend
> H. Larry Townsend
> H.L. "Hank" Townsend

With the exception of when your address contains an apartment number, or the street address makes a typed line too long, it should be written without any abbreviations. Do not use a box number unless you have no other choice. A phone number where messages may be taken is acceptable. Be certain the party who will be answering the phone for you is reliable, however. Bad impressions begin when the person who is supposed to be doing you a favor sounds unfriendly or rude. Do not include your phone number at work, even though you are working part-time. If this is the only way they can reach you and your employer doesn't mind, then adding it to your address is acceptable.

3

3949 Thermopolis Blvd., Apt. 2
Dingbat, Wisconsin 66124
(414) 555-1212
(414) 555-1891   Messages between 12 and 6 P.M.

Refrain from placing two addresses on your résumé. Never use an address in another town when you don't live there, even though you expect to move there in weeks or months. Better to mention your intention in a separate line of type, just below your phone number.

(414) 555-1212
Will be moving to Atlanta in June.

The Opening Paragraph

The opening paragraph of your résumé can be loosely compared to a bold headline in a printed advertisement. While it certainly is not akin to a one-line catchy phrase, nevertheless its primary purpose is to lure the employer into the main body of information about your background, just as the headline of a slick magazine ad entices one to read further. This brings up an extremely important principle about résumé composition: Never for a moment lose sight of the fact that you are *selling* a product, and that product is yourself. That selling begins with the opening paragraph, which must spark the reader's interest; and if it does not do that, it is a failure and wastes valuable space on the sheet of paper that carries your credentials and hopes for a new job.

The Heading: Your opening paragraph needs a heading. Here are six from which to choose:

- Employment Objective
- Job Objective
- Objective
- Professional Objective
- Career Objective
- Introduction

Career Objective is restricted to those who are just graduating from college, or who are changing career fields. Professional Objective

4

Writing the Résumé

is an option for those who are actually in a field that is deemed to be "professional" by the general public (e.g., medicine, law, etc.).

Opening Words: When you know precisely the type of job you want, some ways to begin the sentence are:

- Seeking the position of
- Pursuing the position of
- Desire a position as
- Wish to assume the position of

Next, name the job, using all capital letters. For example:

Seeking the position of FINANCIAL ANALYST.

If you have two different job objectives, make two different résumés. It is tough enough getting across *one* central theme on a sheet of paper, much less trying to juggle two of them. Two job objectives on the same résumé weaken each other. The employer must not be allowed to ask himself, "What does this person really want?"

Maybe you can't identify the *exact* type of position you would like, but you know it is in a certain field. This is often true of new college graduates, as well as those who have been employed but wish to change career fields. You may alter your beginning words to read:

- Seeking a position in the area of
- Pursuing a position in the field of
- Desire to secure a position in the area of

To one of these three (or something of your own), add the name of the employment area or field, capitalizing each letter. For example:

Seeking a position in the field of MANUFACTURING.

Here are some major career fields.

Manufacturing	Health & Fitness	Food Service
Data Processing	Merchandising	Sales
Medical Care	Maintenance	Purchasing

Customer Service	Shipping/Receiving	Criminology
Social Work	Finance	Engineering
Travel	Marketing	Banking
Chemistry	Athletics	Government
Construction	Animal Care	Safety
Education	Advertising	Administration
Real Estate	Security	Transportation
Merchandising	Mechanics	Banking
Computer Science		

If you cannot identify a specific job or career field, then don't. In this case, you would be better off using the heading *Introduction* and shaping your first paragraph into a short summary of your background or credentials. This will be explained later.

Statement of Experience: Some people want to make a general one-sentence statement about their experience to support their objective. Here are four examples:

- I have ten years experience in accounting.

- Have acquired important experience in the area of merchandising and distribution.

- As a recently discharged member of the armed services, offer three valuable years of experience in this field.

- Have served as a co-op in this field for the past two years, gaining hands-on experience while working in the lab of the Procter and Gamble Co.

Knowledge Gained: Your knowledge is the cornerstone of your value to an employer. That's what the employer buys. And if you do not have knowledge in the employer's field, then he may buy your potential; but potential has a very short honeymoon. Before long, the employer who takes a chance on you is going to want *results*. You will be expected to learn and produce. The extreme example of "knowledge gained" could easily be the self-employed individual. She must learn and handle the buying, selling, supervision, administration, advertising, and customer relations that attend small business operations. If the job doesn't get done, sales may be affected; and poor sales usually mean she is out of business. Basically, a one-room shop is a microcosm of a large corporation which would otherwise assign many individuals to each of those areas — areas which the small business owner handles alone, or at least at the outset until she herself becomes highly successful.

The individual who is not self-employed, who is assigned to one department of a large or small company, very often expands his knowledge within that narrow framework as well. For example, an individual in the Accounting Department may gain complementary knowledge in the area of data processing and customer relations. This knowledge becomes a part of that person's credentials when he goes looking for another job. It is the indispensable artwork that one carries into the interview and displays before the hiring employer. Managers who decide to look for a new position often come well-stocked with such knowledge, assuming they became managers as a result of what they knew and had done.

To add information about the knowledge you have gained, begin your sentence with a phrase similar to one of these:

- I have a strong background in
- My experience includes
- Have gained a knowledge in

To this, add the major brushstrokes of knowledge you have gained.

- I have a strong background in bookkeeping, purchasing, and credit.

- My experience includes estimating construction costs; coordinating construction projects; and purchasing raw materials (up to $100K)

- As a result of employment positions held while going to school, I have acquired a knowledge of several administrative aspects which are critical in operating a business. . . .

You may also add information which is even more specific, possibly capable of setting you apart from others who are applying for the same job. It is in fact a special skill (a topic to be covered later) within one branch of knowledge. As someone in the field of administration, for instance, you may have learned a great deal about operating a type of business equipment plus the development of forms, either or both of which could be important to the prospective employer. Here are two examples:

- I have learned a great deal about lubricants and how, with proper maintenance, they may be used to eliminate machine downtime.

- Have acquired an extensive knowledge of investigating and solving the problems of customers.

To help you decide if you have any specific knowledge, you may use this procedure: (1) in the following list of key words, find those which apply to you; (2) finish the sentence, using as brief a statement as possible—two to four words, ideally. More specific information is gained when you take the trouble to respond to the word in parentheses. But before you begin, remember one thing: you are *selling*, not producing an in-depth biography. Therefore, while there are no restrictions on the total amount chosen, ask yourself if it adds important information to your résumé. If it doesn't, don't bother with it.

interviewing (who?)	demonstrating (what?)	planning (what?)
recruiting (who?)	consolidating (what?)	organizing (what?)
advising (who?)	promoting (what?)	installing (what?)
supervising (what? or who?)	distributing (what?)	collecting (what?)
	purchasing (what?)	solving (what?)
investigating (who? or what?)	repairing (what?)	designing (what?)
	selling (what? to who?)	developing (what?)
directing (what? or who?)	counseling (who?)	coordinating (what?)
	teaching (who?)	simplifying (what?)
inspecting (what?)	negotiating (with?)	writing (what?)
estimating (what?)	testing (what?)	operating (what?)

Types of Employers: Your opening paragraph may contain information that characterizes your present or past employers, as well as their approximate size.

- Have been associated with two well-known electronic companies, one exceeding $700M in sales.

- Employers have been Fortune 500 companies whose yearly volumes top $600M.

You must be careful about including information of this nature, however. Making mention that you have had several employers is not appropriate when your work history is short; it makes you look like a "job-hopper." And an employer's sales volume may not be impressive at all to that company which is earning twice as much. For those individuals just getting out of college, or the Army, or who are changing careers, information such as this rarely has any bearing.

Preferences: If you are confident that your background is quite marketable, and should you wish to prevent being bothered by those employers who might contact you to offer you "just another job," stating your preferences in the first paragraph is one of the best ways to avoid this. It would seem to be a luxury that very few job hunters enjoy. But if handled properly, job hunters can use this approach in the opening paragraph of their résumés. The trick is to not be arrogant about it. Therefore, instead of starting off with *Will accept nothing but . . .* or *Demand that . . .*, employ some subtlety.

- Prefer a position which will give me an opportunity to interact with customers regularly.
- Very interested in a position where my planning and scheduling skills may be used effectively.
- Would be especially receptive to employment that would allow me to gain experience with computers.
- Job preferences include solving problems, testing new ideas, and eliminating waste.

By no means should you say anything about wanting a job that will provide you with more money or future promotion. One should assume you would want that without having to say it. Here are some key words which may help draw some of this information out of you. In your notes, write *I want a job where. . .* and then finish the sentence, using one of these words and a very brief explanation. If you use more than six words to elaborate on any of them, you may be overdoing it. And don't worry about the structure right now; just get it down on paper. The editing comes later.

achieve (what?)	develop (what?)	consolidate (what?)
comfort (what?)	eliminate (what?)	begin (what?)
communicate (what?)	negotiate (what?)	develop (what?)
coordinate (what?)	conceive (what?)	purchase (what?)
design (what?)	evaluate (what?)	help (what?)

improve (what?)	repair (what?)	write (what?)
interact (what? with who?)	prevent (what?)	supervise (what? who?)
	conceive (what?)	examine (what?)
reduce (what?)	sell (what?)	research (what?)
research (what?)	simplify (what?)	arrange (what?)
save (what?)	solve (what?)	maintain (what?)
counsel (what?)	study (what?)	control (what?)
organize (what?)	teach (what? who?)	design (what?)
plan (what?)	test (what?)	build (what?)
analyze (what?)		

Personal Profile

This information may or may not earn a separate place on your résumé; it depends on its caliber and the extent of it. More often than not, it is heavily edited down to a couple of lines and placed in the opening paragraph. On the other hand, you may choose to use none of it; but you cannot decide if it will make a valuable addition until you have gone through the following exercise. Basically, the idea behind it is to paint a thumbnail portrait of yourself in terms of innate talents, acquired skills, and character. You are saying, "You should interview me instead of that other person."

The Heading: Assuming for the time being that the information you develop is worthy of a separate category of its own, here are some headings that can be used:

- Personal Profile
- Skills
- Strengths and Characteristics
- Personal Sketch

However, if the information provided is comprised entirely of skills, then "Skills" would be a more appropriate heading to use. Pick the one that you think will suit you best, or develop one of your own. Whichever, you can always change your mind later on.

Skills: "Skills" are the result of acquired experience—as opposed to talents, which are inborn—and they are fused by your own interest, then honed to a sharp edge through practice. Some skills may be applied to many different fields, thereby making them unique in that regard: for example, being adept at using a certain kind of computer software program might allow you to work for an employer who is engaged in developing chemicals, or selling insurance, or manufacturing toys. On the other hand, some skills can only be used by those who are in the same field. Nevertheless, a skill is a career credential that is transferable and, therefore, marketable. To the employer it means that he doesn't have to *train* you to do it. For instance, if you can flip pancakes beautifully for one restaurant, you can surely do it for another. You don't lose that skill by simply changing jobs. Yet, it is a rather common practice for one to go job hunting without ever taking an inventory of his skills. Quite simply, being well-armed with this knowledge gives you another offensive weapon during the interview phase.

Beyond that, such information certainly looks impressive on your résumé. And the more skills you own, the better chance you have of prodding the interest of the employer. Never take a skill for granted, despite the fact that many other people may be equally adept at the same thing. Eliminating it from your résumé may be the very one that interests an employer the most. List only those skills which complement your job objective or career interests. For instance, if you are looking for an engineering position, it will probably do you little good to say that you're skilled at keeping error-free accounting ledgers. A skill must be explained as briefly as possible, although usually exceeding one word. Suppose you say that you can organize. Swell. Organize what? Ducks in a row? Military divisions? See how it leaves the reader hanging in midair? If you can tell what you are good at organizing and how this helps the employer, you can make it even more powerful. (See the example which follows.)

> I am good at organizing people into compatible groups, which results in teamwork, high productivity, and fewer problems.

It is important for to you to understand that quality and quantity of skills do not necessarily increase with age. Their existence is usually dependent upon the education, interests, varied jobs and circumstances, and the number of past employers one has had. Therefore, it is quite possible—perhaps even likely—that a job seeker who is 30 years old and has worked for three different employers may have acquired more skills than one who is 50 years old and has worked for the same company most of his life. New college graduates, for the most part, also have skills—although not extensively.

To determine if you have any skills worth mentioning, write the phrase "I am good at" on your worksheet. Then look at the first word in the first group which follows to see if it possibly applies to you. Do not *make* it apply: the purpose of the exercise is to determine your "strengths," not how many slots you can fit yourself into. Review each word in each category and write as many skills as you think you might have.

> *Something Old:* maintaining, eliminating, preserving, repairing, restraining, modifying, decreasing, adapting
>
> *Something New:* organizing, transforming, planning, inventing, originating, initiating, recommending, writing, creating, testing, designing, developing
>
> *Eyes and Ears:* observing, interpreting, identifying, inspecting, reviewing, listening, defining, investigating, detecting
>
> *Putting It Together:* collecting, acquiring, researching, sorting, assembling, building, forming, editing
>
> *Mental:* remembering, diagnosing, projecting, estimating, calculating, forecasting, evaluating, predicting, judging, appraising, solving, analyzing
>
> *Human Relations:* negotiating, recruiting, mediating, influencing, communicating, interviewing, conversing, advising, entertaining, lecturing, consulting, inspiring
>
> *Leading the Way:* motivating, delegating, promoting, teaching
>
> *Keeping It Going:* scheduling, improvising, administering, expediting, coordinating, processing, generating, controlling
>
> *Monetary:* budgeting, saving

When you are finished jotting down a preliminary list of skills (and there is no limit to the amount you may record), check them over for redundancies. It is easy to say the same thing twice without realizing it. Remember: you are promoting; you are trying to form an immediate impression in the employer's mind.

Talents: You might have been endowed with one or more innate gifts on the day you were born—the kinds of things which, while your friends and associates have always sweated and struggled to achieve a passing competency in some area, you have always been able to accomplish the same thing with remarkable ease. In other words, it comes naturally to you. For our purposes here, we shall call them talents. So, here's the question: Is there something you can do with alarming ease, something you might take for granted, but which you've heard other people say, "I wish I could do that"? If you do, and it is possible the talent may be utilized by your next employer, does it not logically follow that it should be included in your résumé?

Therefore, being endowed with such a talent, write it — or them — beneath the word *Talents*. Here are examples:

- I have a superior memory, enabling me to recall names, dates, and situations with complete accuracy.
- Possess a natural problem-solving talent.
- I make friends with people very easily.

You will edit your information later.

Personal Sketch: Determining how others see you can sometimes be rather important, both from a negative standpoint as well as a positive one. For example, if you are somewhat shy and cannot handle rejection well, then to write a résumé in pursuit of a sales job means you are being unrealistic about what you think you can do. While you certainly wouldn't mention your shyness or fear of rejection on your résumé, it can at least warn you what to stay away from. So, what have they said about you? First, on your worksheet, write the phrase "I'm considered by others to be. . . ." Then, looking at the words which follow, choose no more than three. Too many weaken the effectiveness of the others. With the exception of some words, e.g, creative, enthusiastic, knowledgeable, inventive, versatile, and imaginative, there is no reason to write anything beyond those which you have chosen. Further, use only those which you think will best promote you on paper.

aboveboard	enthusiastic	punctual
analytical	inquisitive	reliable
self-determined	assertive	inventive
cheerful	knowledgeable	versatile
conscientious	open-minded	sociable
considerate	patient	thoughtful
creative	persevering	tireless
positive-thinking	determined	imaginative

Providing a one-line description of yourself as a worker can sometimes be a strong selling point on your résumé. But if you find it difficult to characterize yourself, forget it and go on to the next step. If you choose to respond, write the phrase, "I am the kind of person who," and then finish the sentence. Write no more than one sentence.

> I am the kind of person who can usually bring order out of chaos, as a result of being able to pinpoint the problems causing it.

Education

This is usually a very important part of the new college graduate's résumé; but for the individual with experience, its informational value begins to quickly decrease after that person has been employed. One exception—and there are others—would be those professionals in the field of medicine, where it is commonplace to find them adding to their schooling to keep abreast of new technology. Truly, some seem to go to school for what seems forever. Even at that, it still does not mean that such information should be highlighted by giving it a prime spot on the page.

The Heading: Generally, only one of three headings are used for this category.

- Education
- Educational Background
- Academic Background

Order of Importance: The education which more directly relates to the job you are seeking should be listed first. For instance, say you have a bachelor's degree in sociology. However, you have just completed a 16-week course in restaurant management. Now, as impressive as that college degree may be to some people, it probably won't ring any bells for the person who owns a restaurant and needs a manager. You have got to appeal to him and no one else. Consequently, you would put your restaurant education first and your college degree second. An example:

Writing the Résumé

> Have completed a 16-week course in restaurant management through the Restaurant Management Association.
>
> Received a <u>B.A. in Sociology</u> from Ohio State University in 1981.

In this case, however, the college degree should be underlined as you see above. While the other education is important to your getting a job, you do not want it to completely overshadow something that took you four years to get. Employers tend to skim-read résumés, and the underlining helps to ensure that he *will* see it — as long as the underlining is not excessive. If it is, it defeats the whole purpose.

In most cases, here is the order in which degrees of education should be listed:

1. Doctorate Degree
2. Master's Degree
3. Bachelor's Degree
4. Associate Degree
5. Years of college credits (no degree)
6. Seminars and company courses
7. Military education
8. Correspondence courses
9. High School (rarely included)

College Degree: As an experienced person with one or more college degrees, you should be aware by this time that the more extensive your background, the less impact your education will have on the reader of your résumé. It just doesn't stack up against what you have done and can do. It is a passkey more than anything, opening doors that are otherwise closed to those without degrees. However, depending upon what field you are in, the acquisition of advanced degrees may well be crucially important. Some professionals must continue to go to school out of self-survival. If they don't keep up on the latest things in their fields, they will surely lose a competitive edge and suffer economic hardship along with it. This continuous "adding to the list" can, unfortunately, make the Education portion of their résumés appear to be topheavy, requiring very judicious editing.

As a new college graduate, of course, your education will serve as the "product" of your résumé, as opposed to any experience you may

15

have. Your education is what you're selling. That's not totally true, however. While on the surface it may *appear* that you are selling your knowledge, what you are *actually* marketing to employers is your youth which goes along with it. An employer will pay the price for the right degree and the potential of the person holding it. In effect, you represent new blood, perhaps the keeper of a new idea yet unleashed, and the gamble from his side is largely worth it.

Whether you are experienced or a new graduate, merely list your degrees on your worksheet, the name of the college where they were achieved, and the year in which they were obtained. Unless it is possible that the reader of your résumé might confuse your college with another (e.g., The University of Miami in Florida and Miami University in Ohio), there is no need to include the name of the town where your alma mater is located. Neither is it necessary to include the year when you entered college. The name of your educational institution and your degree, plus the year you obtained it is all that is required. The month is not necessary unless you feel it's important.

College Major: As a job seeker with a college degree, you may include your major if it complements the type of job you are seeking. If it doesn't, don't include it. Suppose you are seeking a job in the business environment, it will likely cause you to be eliminated from consideration if you say that your major was in history. This does not mean that you are not able to hold the position (in fact, you may be more qualified than anyone applying), it simply means that that is the way the game is played. The purpose is to convince them otherwise, but you won't get the chance if you "tell all" up front. Again, a résumé is an advertisement, not a confession. Three examples:

- B.S. Finance, St. Louis University, 1965
- St. Louis University   B.S. Finance   1965
- Arizona State University
  Received a Bachelor of Arts, in History   1980

If you find yourself in the position of changing careers, and you have not broadened the base of your formal education to allow for that change, you will have to determine how much you want the prospective employer to know about your college major. Holders of some degrees of education find it easier than most to accomplish such a switchover; the best example is one who owns a degree in Business Administration, which today has almost become generic and is transferable into so many different areas. The general rule, however, is this: The more *specialized* the education, the harder it is to adapt to a new career — in the mind of the hiring employer, that is. Therefore, your major should probably be eliminated from your résumé altogether. Let the employer ask you about it during the interview. To restate the purpose of your résumé: it is only supposed to get you the interview, not the job. If you cannot convince the employer of your worthiness when you sit across from him, your résumé will certainly not accomplish the task.

College Minor: Minors listed on a résumé have little or no impact on the person who reads your résumé, for the word "minor" speaks for itself. Of course there are exceptions, and your major and minor, in concert with one another, may sometimes make a powerful combination. For instance, if your major was in political science and your minor was in a foreign language, this could well improve the brightness of your star if you were seeking a career in government service. When including it, however, always precede it with your major. If your college minor does not add anything positive to your résumé, there is no point in using it except to help fill the void on the sheet of paper.

Scholarships: Making mention of the scholarships you received is quite acceptable. However, this type of information quickly loses its appeal to the potential employer when you — the job seeker — have already gained experience. Unless it is a truly outstanding scholarship worth noting, it is information generally found only on the résumé of a new graduate. Athletic scholarships should not be mentioned, unless they are pertinent to the job which you are applying for (e.g. coach).

Recording the name of the scholarship, its amount (or what it paid for), and the field for which it was given is the kind of information that is most appropriate.

- Received a $20,000 Economics Institute Scholarship.
- Granted a four-year room and board scholarship by the Educational Foundation of America.

17

- Scholarships: $10,000 from the Brothers of Knowledge.
  $12,000 from the Knights of Old
- Awarded a $10,000, 2-year Yellow Globe Scholarship because of the excellence shown in mathematics while in high school.

Honors: Honors, especially the academic kind, add a nice touch to one's résumé. The more impressive types can remain important for as long as ten years after graduation, and sometimes longer. For example, graduating at the top of your class from a large, well-known college would certainly rank among the more serious contenders. Here are a couple of examples of how it might look on a résumé:

- Received the Lamplight Award for graduating at the top of my class.
- I was given the Faculty Key by the dean of the college, as a result of successfully heading a voter registration drive on campus.

Honors gained as a result of your sports activities are usually not as impressive as academic ones. All begin to pale eventually, however, leaving you to ask yourself if it is going to mean anything to the person who will be reading your résumé, once you are several years out of school. If it will not, then drop it.

Grade Point Average: Should you include your grade point average? Only if it was a good one, meaning 3.0 or better. Although your grade point average in college usually loses its impact the longer you are employed (by then you have far more to prove to the employer than just how well you can pass written exams), it's something that never really goes out of style, and it indicates that you're smart, or a hard worker, or both. You may place your G.P.A. in parentheses, just after your date of graduation. For example:

Xavier Univ.   B.S.   1984 (3.2/4.0)

Or you can place the information on a separate line.

Xavier Univ.   B.S.   1984
—Achieved a 3.2 G.P.A. on a 4.0 scale.

Writing the Résumé

Do you have one good G.P.A. and another one which is only fair? You would be better off not including either, because a lower average always diminishes the one which is higher. This holds true whether you are talking about completely separate degrees, or an overall G.P.A. versus the one received in your major. Don't delude yourself into thinking that if you include the high one and omit the low one that no one will ever notice. They will, because you will have created a mysterious gap of information. Take a look at the example below. If you had placed information under your *Education* heading, the employer could not help but suspect your grades were not very good at New College. That, in turn, creates a negative.

| Akron University | M.B.A. | 1953 (3.7/4.0) |
| New College | B.S. | 1949 |

Dean's List: If you were on the dean's list and you wish to include it on your worksheet, you may want to reconsider such a move if your overall G.P.A. was less than 3.0. Regardless of the circumstances that prevailed, on paper it looks like you worked hard for a few semesters and then sloughed off the rest of the time.

| Ball State University | B.S.E.E. | 1981 (2.5/4.0) |

- Member of dean's list for three semesters

What happened to you during the other semesters? Do not exclude your G.P.A. and include the fact that you were on the dean's list. This only encourages the interviewer to ask about your G.P.A.

College Expenses: Did you pay for all or a portion of your college expenses? Or are you doing so now, while employed and earning a degree? Whether you are a new graduate or someone who graduated a few years ago, this kind of information can represent a nice touch to your résumé. It shows that, while in pursuit of knowledge, you had the grit to balance two major functions in your life. Working and studying at the same time is no small task, and if you do it while raising a family as well, that makes a pretty powerful statement on your résumé. Should this be true in your case, you have every license to brag about it, and you would be foolish not to do so.

Here are three examples of how it may look on your worksheet, the last of which is the simplest of all:

> I earned 60% of my college expenses through part-time work during the school year and full-time employment during the summer.

> I am presently pursuing and paying for a master's degree in economics, at All Night University, while employed on a full-time basis and raising a family.

> Earned 100% of my college expenses.

When to actually begin *excluding* this type of information really becomes a judgment call on your part. If a considerable amount of time has passed — say, three or four years — or it is taking up valuable space that could best be used for something else, that is certainly an indication when it should be deleted.

Individual Courses: Listing the courses you took in college, in most cases, is an absurd waste of paper space.

No Degree: If you have attended college without receiving a degree, you should first determine — considering the type of job or career field you are pursuing — whether or not you will be competing with many people who do have degrees. And if so, will the lack of a degree eliminate any chances you have of getting an interview? Should your answer be "yes," you might want to omit any mention of your education. Remember, a résumé is not a confession, but rather an advertisement. Get the interview: that is its purpose. Why be eliminated before you even get a chance to explain why you can do the job better than anyone else? If you decide to include your educational information anyway, list the names of the colleges you attended — or are presently attending — and beside each, respond to one or more of the following questions:

Is it important that the employer learn what you studied? For example:

> I have completed two years of study in architecture, at Hard College.

Writing the Résumé

Would it help to relate how many credit hours you have accumulated in relation to your major?

> I have acquired 50 credit hours in architecture, at Hard College.

Would it be better to record how close you are to receiving a degree?

> I need only 25 credit hours to achieve a bachelor of arts degree.

Do you want him to know that you are still attending?

> I am pursuing a bachelor of arts at Hard University while working full time, and expect to graduate in about a year.

Would you prefer to only give the years of attendance, because you wish to hide the fact that you attended part-time, etc.?

> Attended Hard University from 1975 to 1977.

This last example may give the appearance of two years of college credits, although you only have one year of credits or less. Using any of the above examples as a guideline — or a combination of them — record the information on your worksheet.

Seminars: Many who write their own résumés will automatically include information about the seminars they have attended. But you must ask yourself this: Will it add any marketable aspect to my résumé which does not already exist? If it does not, why include it? What purpose is being served other than filling up space? Carefully examine the seminar's title, contents, and speaker. First of all, just because you revere the speaker doesn't mean the employer is going to feel the same way. What is the employer going to think of it when he sees it on your résumé? Put yourself in his shoes. Could the wrong conclusions be drawn from the title alone? Could the mere sight of the speaker's name be detrimental? Don't hesitate in dumping a seminar from your résumé if you think it might warrant it.

With this in mind, some examples follow.

- Attended a one-day seminar, titled "Government vs. Business," on October 17, 1987.

- I completed a one-week seminar, entitled "The French Revolution," conducted by chef Pierré DePaul, in August 1985. Emphasis was on the revolution taking place in the development of French sauces, and I gained considerable knowledge regarding their creation and how they enhance certain foods.

- Seminars include the following:
  - "Mass Appeal," Advertising Institute, 1967
  - "Passing the Word," Advertising Institute, 1969
  - "The Big Buck," Marketing Age, 1970

Company and Correspondence Courses: Only list a company or correspondence course when it applies directly to your job objective, or when it supports your other educational pursuits in some way.

The point is to rid your résumé of any information that breaks the continuity of theme — anything in fact that will prevent the reader from being jolted and having to ask himself, "Why in the world did he study *that*?" Such information which has no strong relationship to other information in your résumé is generally worthless, no matter how hard you worked to achieve it and how proud you may be of having done so. For instance, if you are pursuing a job in administration, you must ask yourself how a five-week course in art appreciation which you completed might help you.

Name the company or correspondence course, plus any additional information you think is pertinent and possibly helpful (e.g., the place where it is achieved, the length, and whether or not a diploma, certificate was granted, etc.). Examples:

- I completed a 16-week correspondence course called "Basic Chemistry," through the Technology Institute, and received a certificate in December 1987.

- Company-sponsored courses total over 100 hours and have involved topics in the areas of waste control, machine safety, time management, and industrial hygiene.

Military Education: If you are not fresh out of the military, and your employment is completely removed from what you did while you were wearing a uniform, there is no point in including that part of your education on your résumé. In fact, if you are just getting out of the service and your military education is not even remotely connected with what you plan to do as a civilian, neither should you include it then. Free space on your résumé for information that is *important*. If your formal education while wearing a uniform is pertinent to what you want to do or are doing, however, including it is quite reasonable — that is, until the information gets old; then drop it. Unlike a college degree, education gained while in the army, navy, or air force is not something that earns a spot on every résumé you produce. Eventually, it goes out of style; in fact, much faster than most information.

Some who opted for 20 years in the armed forces and then retire (usually somewhere in their late thirties or early forties) make a terrible mistake by including *all* of the education they received, which can easily fill an entire page. Summarize all of it down to a few lines, keeping in mind who will be receiving it.

Two examples of how your military education might appear somewhere under your *Education* heading:

Electronics, 20 weeks, U.S.A.F.

U.S. Air Force: Basic Electronics, 20 weeks
Computer Repair, 10 weeks
Personnel Management, 5 weeks
Planning/Scheduling, 7 weeks

High School: When your formal education is limited to high school, there is often no need to include that information, meaning that you can eliminate the *Education* portion from your résumé altogether. In today's job market, most employers expect you to have graduated from high school, much like they expect you to have graduated from elementary school; therefore, there is no need to include it. Likewise, if a high school education is all you have, you don't want to draw attention to it in such a competitive marketplace. It is not your responsibility to eagerly volunteer that which you would rather keep to yourself. You are not lying; you are *omitting* information to prevent being eliminated from contention. If omission adversely affects the page length, you may decide to keep it. Get your foot in the door first; sit face-to-face with your interviewer; then talk about your education, as well as why you think you can do the job better than anyone else.

If you are including your high school education and you graduated with a "B" average, place that average in parentheses.

Should you have completed a seminar, company course, correspondence course, etc. that relates to your objective, place it above the line where you list your high school education. But never include information about such extra education and drop any mention of your high school. It tends to make the reader believe that you are not a high school graduate. Be forewarned that the employer may ask why you didn't go on to college. Better have an answer ready.

Book Reading: Do you read *non-fiction* books on a regular basis that add to your knowledge, not only in relation to your own career field but about the world in general (i.e., politics, health, history, art, etc.)? If you do, it presents you with an opportunity to make a powerful statement about it, for it is another form of education. To an employer who may prefer someone who is constantly in pursuit of knowledge and whose interests are not so narrow, information like this on your résumé can be quite impressive. Usually, readers of books are infinitely more interesting because of what they know and what can be learned by listening to them. You don't have to continue going to college to be given credit (in the employer's mind) for having read books.

Even if you keep your reading of books contained to that area which directly affects your career, that too is impressive. Listing their titles on your résumé will not do; only the subject matter is necessary. Here are two examples: the first from a résumé of an individual who has experience in the job market; the second from one belonging to a new graduate.

> Even with the schedule I keep, I read at least one book per week, the topics of which cover almost all subjects, i.e., government, history, engineering, computers, etc.

> Supplementing my coursework with independent studies in the area of market research—which has involved reading a total of twenty (20) books on the subject, written by established professionals in the field—I have gained a solid appreciation of how this activity can mean the difference between the success or failure of a new product.

You are taking a big gamble if you choose to lie about it. If the employer asks you which books you are talking about, you will need titles; and should he have read any of them and you can't discuss them, your chances are slim. It's just as bad when he hasn't, and you still can't talk about them when he quizzes you.

Education Intentions: Is it acceptable to write on your résumé that you *intend* to obtain a certain degree, without ever having completed one credit hour toward it? Unless you are in the process of completing a degree, the answer is no. Nor should you state your intentions when there may be a large time gap.

Employment

Are you currently employed and seeking another position in the same career field? Then this should represent the main portion of your résumé, for it supports your objective, which is stated in your first paragraph. The amount and quality of experience you have gained will make the difference on whether or not an interview is forthcoming. The new college graduate and the career changer are often at a disadvantage here. Either may have the formal training, but lack the hands-on experience which the employer desires. The forcefulness of their résumés can overcome this obstacle.

The Heading: There are several headings to choose from when you are ready to compile information about your work experience. For example:

- Employment
- Employment History
- Employment Background
- Employment Profile
- Experience
- Experience Profile
- Professional Background
- Career Profile

For the new college graduate, all of the above-mentioned headings can be used, as well as these:

- Part-time Employment
- Part-time and Summer Employment
- Summer Employment

- Co-Op Experience
- Unrelated Work Experience

If you are soon to be discharged from the service, use one of the headings from the first group. Never use the word "Military" in it.

Employer's Name: First write the name of your *present* employer (or *last* one if you are now unemployed), including the month and year you were first employed there, plus the date you left if that is the case. For example:

Quick Paper Company, Mar. 1981 to Present

You do not have to include the addresses or phone numbers of your employers, nor do you have to state the name of your immediate supervisor. When one or more past employers have been located in other geographical areas, you may include the name of the town and state after the company's name, followed by the dates of employment. If it makes the line too long, omitting it is quite acceptable.

XYZ Co., Dallas, TX.   Mar. 1981 to Present

There are some job seekers who — being somewhat paranoid about their present company finding out they are exploring the job market — sometimes replace the name of their employer with the words "Present Employer." While this is acceptable, it suggests that you are not being aboveboard, and one can only guess what effect it may have on the person who is reading it.

Job Title: Directly below the name of that employer, write your job title.

A word of caution here. Some job titles are not at all representative of the kind of work one does, and some are almost disparaging (the word "clerk" for instance). Therefore, do not be afraid to change your title to one which more fairly depicts the responsibilities of the job. No one is suggesting that you make yourself vice-president on a sheet of paper, but a secretary can indeed become an *Administrative Aide;* a clerk might be transformed magically into a *Retail Assistant.* If you feel uncomfortable with this little sleight-of-hand, continue to use your old title. You might even weigh the possibility of not even including a title; simply begin relating your job responsibilities. You can break a lot of rules when writing a résumé.

Some larger companies put roman numerals behind titles, such as Paper Pusher I, Paper Pusher II, etc. To the other employer who's hiring, he may well wonder how many levels you are from the top. Simply drop the number.

Salary: Never include the amount of your salary. If the information about your background intrigues the potential employer enough, he will gladly overlook the fact that you did not include the salary information which he requested in the ad. Many employers are simply doing some "bargain basement" hunting, trying to get the most for as little as possible. Others may place help wanted ads not because they have job openings, but because they want to see what others in a career field are earning in comparison to what they are paying their own employees in the same area.

Work Environment: If someone tells you that he is a dispatcher for the B&B Company, what would that tell you? Not much more than the name of the company and his title. But if he writes this:

> The B&B Company is a young company that makes tires for farm tractors and grosses $14M yearly. It has twenty distribution sites in sixteen states, and it has experienced steady growth over the last six years. As a dispatcher, I work in a fast-paced, computerized office which coordinates critical information to the distribution sites daily, requiring long- and short-range decision-making.

Now you are perhaps a bit more impressed.

By giving the reader a "feel" of your work environment, he might better appreciate a description of your responsibilities. Here are some questions, one or more of which you may wish to write the answers to on your worksheet.

> How large is the company?
> What is the annual dollar volume?
> How many employees work there?

What is its shipment volume?
What is its product line or service?
How diversified is it, if at all?
What's been the growth pattern?
How old is it?
Are things fast or slow-paced?
How critical is *your* job to the employer?
How critical is the *department's* role?

These are just a few of the questions that are available to which you may wish to supply answers. The idea is to paint a picture. Even as a college student you may be able to do this. Here is an example of information that has been compiled and edited.

Within this busy retail environment which has experienced steady growth since I joined it in my sophomore year, flexibility is essential—meaning they depend on me to help customers, assume the duties of another at a moment's notice, and watch out for theft.

You don't have to include this information. The reader of your résumé won't even miss it. It is presented here as an option.

Job Description: Usually you have to say something about what you do or did for your employer. But developing information in this area can be awfully tiresome, and just as tiresome to read. Some get this idea that if they don't tell the reader *everything* they do on their job, that the résumé will not be impressive enough. Consequently, many résumés are burdened with unbearably long job descriptions—although rarely a problem for the new graduate whose experience is severely limited. For the person who is changing careers, a long job description would certainly be a waste of time.

Those who attempt to write their own résumés tend to make one of two mistakes when describing their duties with each job: (1) they say too much, or (2) they don't say enough. They hear so many conflicting statements about this portion of the résumé that they are torn between being afraid of boring the reader and not saying enough to kindle any interest. So, what can you do to prevent either of these two situations from occurring?

You should understand at the outset that your job title alone will usually go a long way toward telling the employer what your overall duties are. Do not list everything you do; tell the reader what's important. Therefore, if you are a sales representative, don't waste the reader's time with an assortment of needless phrases, like "make phone calls to acquire new leads . . . develop reports," etc. The employer already assumes you do that. Instead, as a salesman, what are you promoting? What is the size and location of your territory? What kind of customers are you calling on? Is it highly competitive? Again, paint a quick picture of the job so that the prospective employer can easily visualize the environment around you and your relation to it.

Suppose you are a computer programmer, and you want the reader of your résumé to understand the purpose of your position, or how your job fits into the whole scheme of things. You may list things like these:

> I am consistently engaged in developing software programs that will:
> 1. Speed delivery of the company's products to the distribution sites.
> 2. Make automatic corrections in the production system to prevent overruns.
> 3. Alert management of potential safety violations.
> 4. Produce a more cost-effective operation in all areas.
>
> In addition, I have to:
> 1. Communicate with all department heads to gain information and develop ideas.
> 2. Travel to the distribution sites to observe, first-hand, the results of the programs themselves.

You will edit this information later, hopefully producing a lean, tight-fisted paragraph.

Perhaps you find it difficult to stand back, take a look at what you do, and determine what the most important aspects of your job are. You need methods to help you generate information on the page. Here are three options. You may use one, or a little bit of all three.

Option 1: The easiest way is to obtain a pre-written job description that has been developed by your employer. With such a handy document in hand, you are able to read through it and record what otherwise you might have forgotten. The problem with using them as guides is that often the people who compose them have little idea of the scope of the job about which they are writing. They have a habit of either making something sound far more impressive than it actually is, or capturing only a fraction of what is really required to do it. Your goal, obviously, is to get rid of the junk and use only the more pertinent data. Keep in mind that your job may have changed quite a bit since that job description was first written.

Option 2: You may divide your job into large categories, such as planning, purchasing, finance, etc. Once you have decided what they are, on your worksheet write the first category and underline it. Beneath that include everything you do which applies to it, taking nothing for granted. Listing your duties, rather than placing them in one paragraph, will make your editing task infinitely easier later on. For instance:

> <u>PLANNING</u>
> Plan projects and sequence of activities.
> Plan goals concerning quality and costs.
> Plan manpower needs for both shifts.
>
> <u>PURCHASING</u>
> Buy capital equipment that costs up to $1M.
> Negotiate prices and terms.

Option 3: This option requires that you determine your activities by listing those which occur in the morning, going straight through the day until you have exhausted a whole day's pattern. A couple of entries could look like this:

- I check the newspaper every morning to see what kind of ads our competitors are running and the types of specials they're offering.

- I call the accountant to see if there are any problems with receivables.

Continue doing this until you have exhausted every aspect of your job. It merely requires that you do a little digging and record what you remember. While you will no doubt have much information that you cannot use, you can get rid of it during the editing phase. To ensure that you haven't forgotten anything concerning your job, refer back to the words listed under the *Skills* heading in the personal profile section (pp. 10–12). By reviewing them, you may realize there is something else that should be included.

Whichever method you use to describe your present or last job, do the same thing in relation to the other jobs you have held. Employment positions usually decrease in importance the farther back you go. Therefore, it is often quite unnecessary to give each equal attention.

Some job hunters, enamored as they might be over a job they held two or three jobs back, are prone to provide an explosion of information about that particular employment period. The result is that the résumé becomes completely unbalanced, tipping unnaturally in one direction. It's as if the job seeker is saying that nothing has been as good as *that* job, either before or since. A better approach would have been to select a few strong points of that experience.

Knowledge Gained: The question is simple: Did you gain anything while holding that job which could be considered beneficial? An example:

> This job taught me a great deal about customer relations.

Later when reviewing your notes regarding your experience, if you believe the knowledge is worth noting, then it should be included in your résumé; and you may put it with your employment data, or you can add it to your opening paragraph.

Reason for Leaving: Including a "reason for leaving" a particular employer is not generally wise. An exception might occur when an employer went bankrupt, or moved its headquarters. In most cases, however, even that information is not necessary. Giving a reason for leaving an employer often sounds like an "excuse," as if you are trying to smooth over a rough spot in your background. When it seems essential that you say *something* about why you left (or are now leaving) an employer, be as brief as possible in your explanation without sounding bitter. A one-sentence explanation will do.

New Graduate: As a new graduate, the fact that you might feel uncomfortable when writing about your past employment is perfectly understandable. After all, your efforts have been devoted toward getting that degree, leaving you with an opportunity to hold only part-time and summer jobs which may not have any connection with what you want to do.

31

In that light, it is quite common for some to attempt to make their summer and part-time job responsibilities sound more impressive than they actually were. This is unwise.

If you are faced with a situation where your work experience is spotty and unconnected with your career goals, don't feel alone. You happen to be in the great majority of new graduates. Consider just listing the names of your employers, including the dates of employment, in a vertical row. Job titles (if you had any), a description of your duties, and the dates may all be eliminated if you wish. There's no reason to inform the reader of your résumé that you served as a cashier at an all-night truck stop. If they want to know; let them set up an interview where you may relate such information.

PART-TIME & SUMMER EMPLOYMENT

Last Employer and Dates
Previous Employer and Dates
Previous Employer and Dates

If your work experience has been more meaningful, however, see "Job Description," beginning on page 28. Like the full time employee, you usually learn something wherever you work, and saying something about it can often help you. This is an attractive option for any graduate, whether he has had a lackluster work background or one that is more meaningful. For example:

> While holding part-time and full-time jobs to help earn expenses, I was privileged to learn about different aspects of the business world, on account of the positions I held and my own natural inquisitiveness. For example, I gained a sharper insight into how management structures affect the hourly worker; how proper purchasing can be a cost-saver; and how positive customer relations help ensure a company's success.

Co-Op Experience: As a participant in your school's "co-op" program, the experience you acquired is almost always directly applicable to the career you have chosen. As such, its importance should not be underestimated, for you often gain an advantage over the individual who did not co-op and who does not have applicable experience.

In listing your co-op experience, you should follow these procedures: 1) Select a heading from the first group under "Headings" at the beginning of this section (p. 25), or use "Co-Op Experience";

Writing the Résumé

2) Follow the procedures outlined on pages 26–31; 3) Put other jobs under a heading such as "Unrelated Work Experience," for to place your co-op background with meaningless employment is to risk weakening its importance; 4) If you worked as a co-op for the same company *at different time periods*, do not list that company more than once on your résumé. Group all of your co-op experience beneath that employer and separate the experiences by dates. One example:

> General Electric Co.
>
> Have served as a Co-Op three (3) times for this aircraft manufacturer. Specifically, this has included the following:
>
> Sept.–Dec. 1989 Held the position of. . .
> July–Oct. 1988 In the Pattern Department, was. . .
> May–Sept. 1987 Assigned to the. . .

Class Projects: One area that is frequently overlooked by new graduates when compiling the Experience portion of their résumés are those instances when they were engaged in meaningful class projects. These are the times when students, either on their own or in association with a small group, assume responsibility for a special task relative to their career major. As a result, practical knowledge or statistical data through research is gained that proves to be beneficial in some manner.

At the extreme end of such projects have possibly sprung actual businesses which have flourished and become recognized as multi-million dollar moneymakers. (The idea behind Federal Express began as a college student's term paper.) Other projects have no doubt uncovered valuable information that eventually launched books on those subjects, or changed the way a certain segment of people looked at a particular thing or event. These are, of course, the exceptions. But if you have been involved in a class project where you were obligated to apply techniques, imagination, rules and ideas in a similar manner used by other professionals in your field, why don't you put that on your résumé? It is *experience.* Simply because you didn't get paid for it doesn't make it unuseable. A worthy class project can only help your résumé.

Sensing the value one of their class projects may have, some graduates mistakenly put it under the *Education* heading. But there it will got lost amid the shuffle of other information pertaining to your recently-acquired degree. Instead, throw this potentially marketable information under the heading that is marked *Experience* (not *Employment*, because you didn't get paid for it). If you are not a co-op, or if you have not worked where the employer made use of your education, then by all means mention this class project *first*. Get it up front where the employer can see it; don't make him dig for it.

You don't have to identify it as a class project. To say that it was tends to lessen its importance in the eyes of the employer.

1. Use the name of the college as a pseudo-employer. (Remember, the information is under "Experience," not "Employment.")
2. State the purpose of the project.
3. Explain what was done as briefly as possible, writing it for the person who may hire you, not grade you.
4. If knowledge was gained, relate that information, too. In fact, any benefits at all should be made a part of the résumé. Knowledge is synonymous with experience in the job market, for one has to *do* something in order to *find out* that something works or it doesn't. The journey to success—no matter what aspect of business or the technical world it may be—is paved with countless errors and booby-trapped with blind alleys along the way.

Here is an example:

University of Common Sense

I participated in a project with another individual to determine
the need for, and marketability of, capturing the rays of the sun
in hollow plastic tubes to eliminate the need for electric lights.
We began by investigating. . . .

Notice, too, that the word *individual* was used, rather than *student* or *professor*. This helps to keep it from reeking of campus life. Your original notes, however, may look something like this:

Project: To determine the feasibility of capturing the rays of
sun in hollow plastic tubes and eliminate the use of electric
lights. If it worked, to determine its marketability.

People in project: 2

Activities: Built plastic tubes. Determined costs. Conducted
tests.

Result: Idea failed, but we learned that. . . .

Writing the Résumé

Class projects can lend a note of distinction to a new graduate's résumé, one which can make all the difference in being recognized by an employer. The reason is simple: The employer relates more quickly to actual experience than he does to what you have learned while sitting in a classroom, or by taking notes in the library.

Career Changer: For someone who is changing careers, it is often best to be stingy in the amount of information you include about those jobs which you have held, for the odds are pretty high that none of them will have any relevance to what you want to do. Say you're a bookkeeper. But now, for some reason, you decide you want to become a sales representative. You are faced with one obvious question: What good is it going to do to describe all of the duties you engage in as a book-keeper? Does the sales manager need someone who can balance the books? No, he needs someone who can sell. So, a detailed description of what you do on a day-in, day-out basis will bore him and will cost you any chance you may have had of getting an interview. This is the dilemma that virtually all career changers face: how to make one's past work experience relate to an entirely different career field. Very often one can't.

One way to attempt to waltz around this problem is to describe how your past experience, although unrelated to the kind of job you're after, has helped to *prepare* you for your newly chosen career. Hence, this same bookkeeper in search of a sales position may write:

> In addition to the normal duties associated with my job, I have been involved in extensive communication with clients over the phone and in person, and on many occasions I have visited potential accounts in the business community, in an effort to solicit their business.

When you are unable to find anything worthwhile, you are often better off by just naming your employer(s) and the dates you worked there. Ask yourself: "What am I selling?" "To whom am I selling it?"

Entering Civilian Life: When you are fresh out of the military, you may feel, perhaps with strong justification, that your experience is not immediately adaptable to a civilian job. If this should be the case, say as little about what you actually did in the service as you possibly can. In fact, you don't have to say *anything* in that regard if you don't want to, but you should say *something*. And that "something" may entail information about what you think you gained from the experience. You can write, for example, about how the three- or four-year span helped shape your character, the values you learned, the broadening of interests it provided, etc.

On the other hand, assuming that you *do* want to talk about the job responsibilities you held while in the service and that you want to place them on your résumé in a manner that will generate interviews in the civilian job market, then refer back to pages 26 through 31. Also as an additional memory jogger, take a look at the words listed on page 12. Perhaps one or more of them will remind you of something.

Refrain from using military jargon. While the person who interviews you may have been in the army or navy himself, there's a solid chance that he's forgotten most of that language.

Record your service dates, using only month and year as you would any period of employment, and refrain from using the word "discharged," followed by a date. Your final date says the same thing.

Military Rank: Never place your military rank on your résumé. If you tell someone what rank you held in the military, they immediately form some impression of you, which is often unfair. Not only is there a chasm between officers and enlisted men, but resentments are even harbored between two- and three-stripers, between captains and colonels, and so on. It is simply another form of prejudice, born out of tradition that is fueled by bunkhouse stories and bolstered perhaps by one or two of our own personal experiences when we once wore the uniform. Where does this leave you? Fairly naked and unable to protect yourself against the prejudice that may be residing inside the person who reads your résumé.

Achievements

Above all the information you might include on your résumé, an achievement can become a peak on a sheet of paper that rivets the employer's interest. It acts as an allure, and it can significantly elevate your value if you can tell the reader how you made or saved your employer money — or how you made things better in some way. With the exception of the government and some non-profit organizations, making and saving money is what interests employers most. An achievement shows that you improved matters, whether it is monetary or not. On a résumé it is usually work-related, though community-related achievements are sometimes acceptable. An obvious *benefit* must be seen to have been derived from it.

However, that benefit cannot be felt only personally; it must be shared by people other than yourself for it to be truly called an achievement.

The Heading: If you have more than one achievement and you wish to place them in a category by themselves to highlight them, there are really only two headings that are acceptable for this purpose.

Achievements
Accomplishments

"Nonachievements": Losing weight, being promoted, and good attendance cannot be classified as your achievements; no one else really benefits. The key in determining whether an achievement can be claimed or not is to determine who benefits from the action taken. The more people who benefit, the greater the achievement.

Method 1: Divide each job you have held into "major components." For instance, beginning with your present or last job, let's suppose it is comprised of *order processing, purchasing, customer service* and *billing.*

Take one of those components and examine every facet of it, to determine if you have done anything which benefited your employer in some way. Perhaps, as you isolate the "order processing" component and begin analyzing what you have done in that area, you remember devising a new inventory control method. You write this:

Devised an inventory control method.

It is not what you *do* that is important, however; it is what *happened* as a result of your doing it that truly matters.

You could expand on it like this:

Devised an inventory control method that saved raw materials.

The more specific you are when writing about an achievement, the

37

better off you are. It provides far more impact on the mind of the person who reads your résumé. For example:

> Devised an inventory control method that saved more than 35% in raw materials.

Use either dollar amounts or percentages when making your calculations; and a calculation is quite appropriate, since rarely can anyone be exact. Further, percentages represent a universal language, and their use is often preferable to dollar figures, unless the monetary amount itself is quite impressive. If, for instance, you had generated more than a million dollars for your employer, you may want to say it like that. But imagine that you had saved your boss $10,000 in the purchase of spare parts, which represents a 20 percent savings. And suppose you opted for the dollar figure:

> Saved at least $10,000 in the purchase of spare parts, by developing new suppliers and initiating bulk shipments.

While that may look impressive when you review the first printed copies of your résumé, to the large company whose purchasing figures exceed two million dollars, you are suddenly talking pittance. However, change it to 20 percent and that same person who reads your résumé automatically replaces the figure by comparing it to his company's purchasing efforts. Now it is 20 percent of two million dollars. To him, the final savings represent $400,000, because he is using his own money as a basis. You haven't done a thing but replace the dollars with percentages.

It is acceptable to use such words as "about," "approximately," and "in the neighborhood of" prior to stating a percentage or dollar figure.

There are some achievements, however, that may have to be written in general terms, primarily because there is just no way you are able to tie either a monetary figure or percentage to the result. These become achievements with only vague results attached to them. They are better than *no* accomplishments. For example, it is extremely difficult—if not impossible—to attach a figure to improved customer service.

> Recommended the policy of accepting phone inquiries in the evening, which significantly improved customer service.

Writing the Résumé

Continue to analyze each major component of each job, beginning with your last employment and working backwards, until you have exhausted them all.

Method 2: This method requires the review of key words, the purpose of which is to jog your memory concerning what you have done that has made something better. It is important that you isolate one job at a time when reviewing each of the following words. Tie a *result* to it.

Before reviewing the columns of words, take a look at these examples.

Did you do something *new?*
(Example: I developed a new advertising campaign that produced 30% more in sales.)

Did you *change* something?
(Example: Reduced manhour expenses by 20%, by updating personnel procedures.)

Did you *manage* something?
(Example: Negotiated a contract with the union that favored the company in all ways.)

Did you *find out* something?
(Example: Uncovered $100,000 in waste through an investigation conducted on my own.)

Did you *express* something?
(Example: Recommended that the company enter the slate business, which generated over $50,000 yearly in profit.)

Did you *help* someone?
(Example: Taught English to disadvantaged youths on a part-time basis, 75% of whom went on to college.)

Use these words:

adapt	direct	investigate
advise	discover	maintain
analyze	divert	mediate
apply	eliminate	modify
arrange	fix	negotiate
classify	identify	organize
compile	improve	originate
consolidate	increase	plan
convert	initiate	predict
create	install	prepare
design	integrate	propose
detect	introduce	recommend
develop	invent	recruit

39

replace	streamline	teach
research	strengthen	test
simplify	study	update
solve	systemize	write

Miscellaneous

What appears in this section are merely options; in fact, a couple will probably surprise you. But they are presented to give you every opportunity to advertise yourself through your résumé.

Testimonials: There is absolutely nothing wrong with putting testimonials on your résumé. But where do you get them?

Start by looking to see if you can find a glowing performance report stuck away in a drawer somewhere, one which came from a past or present boss. Or can you get your hands on a letter of thanks sent to you by a customer who was appreciative of the services you rendered? How about past letters of reference? You may extract one or two sentences that extend no more than three typewritten lines on your résumé.

Write the word "Comment" on your worksheet and underline it (add an "s" if you have more than one testimonial). From one of the sources which you have found, extract whatever information you think will help sell you. Provide the name of the person who wrote it, including that individual's title (if impressive) and the name of the organization with which he was associated at the time the praise was written. Place quotation marks at the beginning and end of each quote. Do not date the quote, and use no more than two. When eliminating words within the quote for reasons of space, insert an ellipsis (. . .). If you end a quote before the sentence truly stops, place an ellipsis (. . . .) after the last word and add an extra period (.).

<u>Comments</u>

- "He alone can take credit for introducing our company to a totally new market, allowing us to remain competitive."
  —Adam Jones, VP of Operations
  Smith Tool Company

- "Thanks so much for your concern and patience . . . which we found surprising and refreshing. . . ."
  —Vera Stiller, Customer

- ". . . [Jim] quickly created outlets for our products, generating a 35% increase in sales, and [he] was a high producer . . . We would like to rehire him."
  —Jack Kerns, President
  XYZ Corp.

The first example shows a quote that is intact. The second illustrates one where some words have been removed to comply with space limitations, but the meaning has not been altered. The third shows that not only have words been removed, but some have been substituted and placed in brackets, not parentheses, for the sake of identifying or clarifying something.

It is essential that you make copies of the entire contents of the correspondence from which you are pulling comments for your résumé. When you are invited for an interview, the chances are good that the employer will ask about the comments you included. If you cannot substantiate them with copies of the original, their credibility is diminished!

Work Philosophy: Do you have a personal work philosophy that tells the employer something about the way you approach your job? Assuming you do and you believe it is important enough to include on your résumé, write "Personal Philosophy" on your worksheet and underline it. Beneath it state your philosophy, and keep it short. A one- or two-sentence statement is about the limit.

Personal Philosophy

I believe that an individual has an obligation to perform in his job as if he owned the company himself.

Stay away from trite phrases (e.g., "When the going gets tough, I get going," etc.), and don't put yourself through the agony of trying to come up with an entry when you don't feel strongly about something. To do so is to invite words that will, taken as a whole, have a hollow meaning to the reader. That's far worse than not writing anything at all. Further, keep in mind that the chances are good that you won't even have space to include this information, even though you think it has merit. Yet, at this stage of your résumé development, it is better to have it than not. It, like everything else in the *Miscellaneous* category, is found on the second page of a résumé, although in some instances it can even be placed in the opening section.

Hobbies and Interests: This category is often worthless, if not flat-out dangerous. You rarely have the slightest idea who is going to be reading your résumé. You don't know if the individual hates tennis players, fired a lazy coin collector, or has a personal vendetta against opera buffs. He is a complete stranger to you, and you aren't familiar with his various prejudices, regardless of how ill-founded they may be.

And even assuming the reader of your résumé has been shorn of any prejudices and pet peeves; what good is served by telling him or her something which has virtually no relation to the job you are after?

Memberships: This category should also be eliminated unless it relates directly to the type of position you are seeking. It is often dangerous to identify yourself with certain groups, especially political or religious ones.

For the most part, your memberships aren't going to make any difference at all when it comes to someone respecting what you have to offer. There *are* exceptions, depending upon the type of career one has. Suppose you are an architect and you belong to a group that is dedicated to the preservation of historic landmarks. Including that information on your résumé could possibly work to your advantage.

If you wish to include one or more, and you hold a position of responsibility, the latter should be added as well. Further, if you feel your duties support or show another dimension of your capabilities, include them also. Place all of them in the order of what you think the employer might deem important.

<u>Memberships</u>

Member and Social Chairman of Better Health Care for Senior Citizens, which requires planning about five social functions per year, averaging more than 200 guests each, for the purpose of raising funds to initiate new legislation.

Activities: This should not be confused with memberships or interests. You may, for example, be actively engaged in something without being a member or having great interest in it. After all, contributing your time toward something could be borne out of a sense of obligation rather than interest.

Writing the Résumé

But this information, too, can be dangerous when included on your résumé. While you may possibly be a member of a group without ever doing anything more than paying your yearly dues and carrying a card which proves that you belong, an "activity" demands actual involvement in something, even if sporadic. A negative answer to any of the following questions should cause you to pause before adding the activity to your résumé: Is it free of any prejudice on the part of the reader? Does it complement you in some manner? Is it closely connected to the career you are in or are seeking?

Whether you choose to follow the advice just set down is strictly your decision, but you should be warned that religious and political activities can be explosive in the mind of the reader. Further, what you deem to be an important part of your life often has almost nothing to do with promoting you on a sheet of paper.

New Graduate: Unlike the job hunter who has some experience under his belt—whether he or she is staying in the same career or is attempting to make a change—the activities of the new college graduate can play a more important role on the résumé.

Beyond the fact that a new graduate's past school activities can also act as a "space filler," there are some cases—depending upon their nature and what was actually done—where they can actually give one applicant an edge over another. For instance, if you are entering the field of business and you were a member of the Business Club on campus, that can only be a mark in your favor. Moreover, if you were president or held some impressive-sounding title within that club, that's two marks for your side. And if, as a result of your participation, the club actually *did* something that was noteworthy in relation to some aspect of business, it is well worth noting.

> I was a member of the Business Club for three years, and served as president during my senior year. Under my leadership, we launched a highly successful auction on campus to provide funds to pay for one-day visits of successful entrepreneurs. This will now be an annual event.

Something of this nature would be better placed under the heading of *Achievements*.

The standard guideline regarding your activities is this: The more closely related it is to your intended career, the more highly regarded it usually is. But this doesn't mean that you should forget the others. In the eyes of the employer, *all* of your activities may help draw a portrait of your character. Offices held within fraternities and sororities are rarely worth noting. For the most part, the same goes for sports, intramural or varsity.

Awards: These are nice, especially if they are career-related. Simply write "Awards," underline it, and beneath it write the name of the award and when it was received beneath it.

> Awards
> Named "Houston's Business Woman of the Month" in August 1989.

Mention only the important ones and don't attempt to explain why you received them. Leave it to the employer's imagination.

Personal Statistics: The practice of including personal information has dogged the overwhelming majority of résumé that are prepared, and some attention must be paid to it at this point. Such information is rarely, if ever, marketable. It has the potential of working against you, depending on management's prejudice with regard to age and the like. A résumé, no matter how well it is written, cannot reflect your enthusiasm, your dedication, your poise, or any of several qualities that can only be discerned by a face-to-face meeting. A résumé can only *advertise* you; it cannot, however, *sell* you. That chore rests squarely on you during the personal interview. Therefore, if you put information on your résumé which robs you of the interview, you lose the chance to sell yourself.

Nevertheless, if you are intent on including your personal information because you feel that you must, write "Personal Information" or "Personal Statistics"; then choose all or some of the following:

> Date of birth
> Height
> Weight
> Marital status
> Number of children
> Ages of children

Writing the Résumé

With the exception of your date of birth, which should have the abbreviation "DOB" before it, there is no point in writing the words "Height," "Weight," and "Marital Status" before their entries.

Personal Information
DOB: Feb. 2, 1961   6'1"   180 lbs.   Married

Past Military Background: Except in those instances when you have just been discharged and must account for the last two to four years of your life, or you received a noteworthy commendation (Medal of Honor through Bronze Star), your military background has practically no influence on the employer whatsoever. If you feel compelled to include information about your military experience, make it simple. Put it with the information about your date of birth and height, etc. Don't say what rank you attained. An example:

U.S. Army, 1972–74

Publications: Have you written anything that has been published, something that has a direct bearing on your career field? If so, you'll want to include it. Write "Publications" and underline it. If you have had an article published in a periodical or newspaper, state the name of the article first and place quotation marks around it. The name of the publication in which it appeared should be underlined or italicized, followed by a comma and the date it appeared.

"Systems for Everyone" *Electronic Highlights*, February 20, 1981.

When you have had a book published, underline or italicize the title, name the city in which it was published, followed by a semicolon, the name of the publisher, a comma, and the year it was published.

The Roar of the Crowd. New York, N.Y.; Lincoln Press, 1984.

It is also acceptable to provide a one- or two-sentence description of the publication. Record your books or magazine articles in the order of their importance, as you see them.

Salary Requirement: Do not include your salary requirement. You will never know if a great job passed you by—one which would have given you the freedom you desire and eventually allowed you to make the money you now want, and far more—all because your salary demand seemed a little high. Your résumé does not begin the negotiating process; it only advertises.

References: Unless you can list a very important person, references are normally useless. Any employer knows that whoever is listed on your résumé will praise your virtues. If you are in tune with that logic, and if you believe that the employer knows that you will supply names and addresses of people who will vouch for you, you may simply write "References Furnished Upon Request" on your worksheet, capitalizing the first letter of each word, with the idea that you will even drop *that* off the final draft if you don't have room for it.

If you feel you must name references, write the word "References" and underline it. Below that, list the name of the reference, his title, the name of the place where he works, and his address and phone number.

References
Jack Spratt, President of More & More Motors,
22 Glen Street, Inch, Oh. (614) 221-6686

Three references are sufficient; and the more impressive, the better. Character references from your physician, teacher, priest, next-door neighbor, and others who are not engaged in the career field that you are pursuing can be looked upon as a complete waste of time.

Editing Your Résumé

Deleting, rephrasing, shifting, emphasizing, regrouping, and adding to a pile of information already amassed is the very backbone of editing. For the nonwriter, it can be a matter of extreme frustration.

Effective editing of your notes first demands that you understand what you are selling; if you do not know that, your information cannot be organized in a manner to produce a central theme. Secondly, you must accept the fact that not all of your information is going to work, that some of it should not be included. Finally, be aware that you will probably have to rewrite it several times (you never will be completely happy with it, by the way), and understand that you will always feel that you have left something out.

An Overview

Information, whether fictional or otherwise, must be polished before it is handed to the reader. It is an integral part of the writing process. Editing requires some understanding of grammar and punctuation; if you are weak in this area, get a book on those subjects from your public library. You don't have to study them as you did in school; just keep them handy when you have a question. Or you have another alternative: cut, combine, and convert as you like, then give it to someone with grammar and punctuation skills. Don't let that individual talk you into changing anything else. The decisions concerning the order, content, and design of your information rests on *your* shoulders. Use them for *their* expertise in grammar and punctuation.

There are several steps that are a part of editing your résumé.

What Are You Selling?

Answering this question is quite important in the editing of your résumé. While your response is not placed on the page itself, the idea of it should be present, thereby leaving the employer no doubt about what you are offering.

To this, the new college graduate may say, "All I've got to sell is my degree, just like most everyone else who is graduating this year." In fact, the new graduate, the career changer, and the individual just getting out of the military may easily find themselves perplexed when it comes to identifying their central sales feature. It is easy to feel disadvantaged when placed alongside the person who has a few years of solid experience in the field of their choice. This is when a knowledge of your skills, your natural talents, your traits come into play, however. If, for example, you are analytical, then evidence of it should be woven into your résumé at various points. If you excel at developing positive human relations, that should be witnessed among the lines you type on the page. It should be done in a manner that is obvious to the reader. A one- or two-page résumé which is only an accumulation of facts and dates will only do you a disservice.

What do you have to offer this employer?

I am selling my ten years experience in inventory control.

Put it aside for future reference. This will *not* be used on your résumé; it will only act as a reminder to you regarding what you feel you are promoting during the editing process. As you whittle away at your information, it would be wise for you to compare your first draft with that small piece of paper on which you wrote what you *thought* you were selling. Do they correlate? If not, does it mean that you were wrong about what you *thought* you were selling, or did you *lose sight of it* and forget to promote it? Should you find the former to be true, you have no alternative but to pitch your previous notion and rewrite your advertising message. In either case, rewriting is necessary.

Editing a résumé is an attempt to leave a clear image in the mind of the employer. If he can't quickly discern what you have to offer, what is to prompt him to spend his time to find out? There are too many other people out there vying for the same job. So, without a solid understanding of what you have to offer, you are at a strong disadvantage when trying to develop a sketch of yourself on paper.

Finally, keep asking yourself such things as: Is this information important? Could it be said better? Am I saying the same thing twice?

Deleting: First, get rid of all the excess words among the information you have assembled. An example:

> ~~I am~~ responsible for managing a $10,000 budget.
> ~~I am responsible for~~ hiring employees.
> ~~I am responsible for~~ ordering supplies.

Now, by inserting a couple of commas and adding the conjunction *and*, you have a series of responsibilities in one sentence.

> Responsible for managing a $10,000 budget, hiring employees, and ordering supplies.

You can reduce that even more.

> Manage a $10,000 budget, hire employees, and order supplies.

As you can see, you can continue to chop away at what you have written until it is quite lean, without losing the main thought. It is a procedure that you should employ on all your notes before thinking about rewriting them. Doubtlessly, there will be many more deletions as you move toward your final draft of the résumé. However, it wouldn't be a bad idea for you to run your notes through a copying machine before you begin deleting words, just in case you get rid of a word that you wish you hadn't.

Combining: Words or phrases may be joined with those from the same section, or combined with those from a different section, as long as they are compatible in some way. Suppose you had designed systems and devices for one employer, but for another you designed exchangers, conveyors, and tools. By combining them, you may summarize your design experience in one line and place it in the introductory paragraph of your résumé.

> Over a 10-year period, have designed systems, devices, ex-
> changers, conveyors, and tools for industry.

Combining words or phrases serves to economize, just as deletion does. It is done to draw attention to a particular aspect of one's background, or to show the *extent* of your knowledge or experience.

Redundancies: Some words and sentences on a page are obviously redundant. A word is used too often, or a sentence says the same thing as one which has preceded it. On review, these are often easy to spot and should be eliminated from the text.

But there are other types of redundancies. For instance, while a key word may not be duplicated, it may be *implied* several times. And instead of respecting the reader's ability to assume a few things himself, related items of no special importance are strung out in a boring series. In the following example, "supervision" is only mentioned once; however, it is implied throughout:

> Involved in overseeing all of the young people who were be-
> tween the ages of 7 and 10 years old. Supervised them at
> school, while they were eating or playing, and at church. This
> was done to make sure a proper code of conduct was main-
> tained individually, as well as at the group level.

The previous example can be edited and rewritten.

> Supervised youths, ages 7 to 10, in all activities to ensure
> proper conduct.

And even *proper conduct* is redundant, for why would anyone take the time to supervise them if not for that? So we can shorten it even more.

> Supervised youths, ages 7 to 10, in all activities.

But if their ages hold no significance, that too could be dropped.

> Supervised youths in all activities.

Once the redundancies and other unimportant information have been dropped, you can see that very little is left. A simplicity of information has been achieved.

Order of Importance: It is also a part of editing to place items within a paragraph in the order of their importance. It is essential that the employer not have to wade through some information to get to what may be termed "the good stuff." Therefore, besides a one- or two-word introduction (even that can be eliminated if you like) begin no paragraph with second rate information, trusting that the employer will faithfully read every word. He won't, and you will lose.

If you have a hard time deciding which information in a paragraph should go first, second, third, and so on, list the items vertically on a separate sheet of paper. For example:

Responsible for:
1. Devising training programs
2. Developing sales strategies
3. Performing market analysis
4. Conferring with ad agency to create company "image"
5. Directing the dispersal of co-op monies
6. Communicating with buyers

By reviewing your list, perhaps you decide their order of importance is as follows:

Responsible for analyzing the market and developing sales strategies. This requires communicating with buyers, devising training programs, and directing co-op monies. Also conferred with ad agency to help create a company "image."

Listing items this way can often be advantageous when deciding what to group together. Could "Responsible for" be eliminated? Of course. If you were writing about your present job, the first word would be "Analyze." But should you be writing about a former position, you would have added an *ed* to it.

Added Words and Phrases: You may add words at the beginning of sentences to improve the flow.

After that, there was no longer a problem. . . .
In addition, was accountable for. . . .
While employed here, increased. . . .
Moreover, maintained a. . . .
Previously, the company had. . . .

51

During this period I. . . .
Within this framework, all. . . .
Since then it has. . . .
For example, no department. . . .
Subsequently, there was a decrease in. . . .

When describing yourself, the word that introduces such information is almost always either an adjective or a verb.

ADJECTIVE: *Capable* of. . . .
Solid experience in. . . .

VERB: *Possess* excellent communication skills.
Have demonstrated an ability to. . . .

When describing what you have done, the word that introduces such information is almost always a verb.

Initiated a way to. . . .
Was accountable for *directing.* . . .

Opening Paragraph

Choosing the Tense: The job objective portion of the opening paragraph is always written in present tense. The same is true when you make any mention of your total experience, skills, preferences.

Definite Objective: Now, as a result of adhering to the procedures found earlier in this book, let us imagine that you have a *definite* job objective, and you have this information available for your first paragraph:

Definite Objective:	Administrative Assistant
Years of Experience:	12 in office management
Areas of Experience:	Bookkeeping
	Purchasing
	Credit
	Systems development
Skills:	Identifying administrative needs
	Expediting paperwork
	Solving problems

Editing Your Résumé

Achievement Summary:	Saved my present employer more than one million dollars through the development of new programs.

After juggling the pieces around and rewriting it several times, you finally use this as a part of your first draft:

> Seeking a position as an ADMINISTRATIVE ASSISTANT, offering more than 12 years of experience in office management, which includes a solid knowledge of bookkeeping, purchasing, credit, and systems development. Quite skilled at identifying administrative needs, expediting paperwork, and solving problems. Have saved my current employer more than $1 million through the development of new programs.

Whether your opening statement is one word or fifty is not the issue. It is what you feel comfortable with and how you think the employer is going to react to what you have written that counts. If two words will "sell you," then use two words. If it takes more, then write more.

Identifying a Career Field: The steps for developing an opening paragraph which identifies a career field instead of a specific job are not any different. You must still chop away, combine, etc. to achieve a tight construction of words. For example:

Major Field:	Sales
Skills:	Human relations
I want a job where:	My monetary gain depends upon my own effort and not because I got a promotion, or because it was an annual thing.
Traits:	Eager, aggressive, self-directing

Out of this may come something like:

> Pursuing an opportunity in SALES. Would like to become associated with a firm which needs an individual who is self-directed, eager, and profit-motivated, with solid human relations ability.

53

Another example of an opening paragraph pointed toward a career field is shown here.

Specific experience:	Sales, purchasing, merchandising, inventory control, and advertising
Years of experience:	10 years
Major field:	Retail
Knowledge gained:	Products Marketing
Types of past employers:	Department stores Distributors
Skills:	Work well under pressure Planning Scheduling

From those notes could come something like this:

Have acquired experience in the areas of sales, purchasing, merchandising, inventory control, and advertising over a 10-year period in the RETAIL field. Have gained valuable product and marketing knowledge while working for major department stores and distributors. Interested in using this expertise in some rewarding position. Work well under pressure, and known to be an excellent planner and scheduler.

Notice that the writer has not told the employer *exactly* what he wants (primarily because he doesn't know himself). All he has done is open the door to his career on a sheet of paper and asked the employer to walk around and see if he can find anything he likes. In effect, he is saying, "I want something in this field, and here are some things I have done while in it. Do you have anything that matches my qualifications?"

Unclear Objective: Without a definite position or major field as an objective, you are forced to deal in a lot of generalities, and employers are asked to read more into your qualifications than they are normally willing to do. This problem should indicate to you that you are in somewhat of a bind, career-wise.

When you are young, indefinite objectives aren't really that serious. As you grow older, however, you cannot afford the luxury of not knowing what you want to do with your life. In any case, what should you do when you find yourself in such a predicament? The solution is to survey your skills very carefully. More often than not, you will find many of them leaning in one direction—in other words, they will feature a preference for working with people, or paper, or whatever. Finding the thread which ties most of them together is not easy. Giving it a name can be even harder, with perhaps *human relations* being the one most commonly used. It is placed in the first sentence of your opening paragraph, in order to set the tone for the rest of the information, which must be highly supportive.

> Seeking a HUMAN RELATIONS-oriented position with a quality company, and would be receptive to discussing employment which requires heavy communication with people on a regular basis. This may involve interacting with an employer's customers or with other individuals.

Almost a Definite Objective: There is another kind of objective that names neither a definite job nor a career; it is sort of in-between. Take, the words "Business Manager." While this is indeed a title which some employers hang on some of their managers, by and large it is a generic term. Such managers wear many different kinds of titles and are found in various departments. Those who fit this mold could possibly do themselves a disservice if, on their résumés, they restricted themselves to a specific job (say, vice-president of marketing) or to a broad career field (e.g., engineering)—primarily because their business background allows them to adapt to so many different kinds of environments.

Should you find yourself in a situation similar to this, and you wish to keep as many doors open as possible, your task will be to name that generic area in a manner that everyone will understand. Such generic terms might include "Production Manager," "Engineering Manager," "Computer Scientist," etc. Here is an example, using "Business Management" as the term.

> Presenting a multi-faceted BUSINESS MANAGEMENT background, and would like to discuss potential employment with a company that needs a decision-maker who can provide fresh ideas and new, positive directions. Possess superior abilities regarding new product implementation, the modification of operations to keep pace with technology, and departmental organization. Have saved my present employer over $50,000 through cost-saving programs that I have developed and implemented.

55

Skills, Traits, and Talents

This information is always written in the present tense. Innate abilities (talents) should be classified as such, but it is important that they stand off from the skills which you acquired during your career.

> Have an exceptional ability in developing systems that work; and have acquired skills in the areas of . . . .

Traits, too, should be set apart in a sentence by themselves, for that is how other people see you, and they should come after both talents and skills.

> . . . eliminating unnecessary paperwork. Generally viewed as an economy-minded professional who can be counted on to bring projects in under budget.

But here is a case where the traits are placed in a series, followed by the person's skills — all in the same sentence.

> Enthusiastic, conscientious, and positive-thinking, and can organize to create efficiency, as well as ensure repeat business through good customer relations.

A trait may also be turned into an adjective which precedes your job classification in the opening paragraph.

> Presenting the background of a *highly imaginative* GRAPHIC DESIGN ARTIST who . . . .

And skills can be listed as part of a series, or divided into separate groups. Italics added here for emphasis; they are not needed in your copy.

> Series: Have proven to be quite skilled at *quickly grasping new software programs,* as well as *teaching their principles to others; coordinating paperwork through various government departments;* and *developing new ideas.*
>
> Groups: Skilled in the area of *project control and coordination.* Moreover, very adept at *design and development of new products.*

Simply insert your skills, traits, or talents wherever you think they will do you the most good. On the other hand, should you possess one that cannot support what you are seeking, then why even contemplate using it? Why jeopardize your chances of landing a good job when it has virtually no relationship to the position you may be seeking?

For the person who is in the process of writing his own résumé, editing one's skills can be a somewhat painful venture. What should be taken out? What should be left in? What kind of "image" do you want to portray? If you answer the last question, you will also gain the answers to the first two. In editing and rewriting your skills prior to the final draft of your résumé, looking at them through the eyes of a possible employer would help immensely. To do so not only provides guidance on deciding what to eliminate — if anything — but also in what *order* to place them. Their order is your final consideration. To you, perhaps all of your skills are equally important, and you have a tough time putting one above the other. Thinking of an employer and what *he* considers to be the most vital to the operation of his company will go a long way toward helping you make that decision.

Education

When writing about your education, use present tense if you are still going to school, but write it in past tense if you are not. Earlier you were told that your education should be listed in the order of its importance, the idea being that you don't want to make the reader wade through the insignificant to get to the significant. However, do not mistake this to mean that you should go through all of your degrees, seminars, and company courses and put *all* of them in the order you think is the most important. That would not only be quite difficult in many instances, but also totally confusing to the reader when he looks at them. When the occasion does arise, it is almost always concerned with the placement of *one* particular type of education before all the others, the rest of which follow the normal pattern as outlined, with your college degree(s) prominent enough to catch the employer's attention. Otherwise, editing the information about your education is easy, with the big decision wrapped around how you want it to look on paper.

Utah State Univ.   B.S.B.A.   1988

Utah State University
  — B.S. Bus. Admin. 1988

Bachelor of Science in Business Administration
from Utah State Univ. in 1988.

B.S.B.A., Utah State Univ., 1988

Received a B.S. in Business Administration,
Utah State University, 1988.

No Degree:

Have completed two (2) years of study in Finance at Williams
College, 1986 to 1988.

Two years of FINANCE, Williams College

Working towards an Associate Degree in Accounting at
Pickens College. Expect to graduate in 1991.

Abbreviations: Abbreviations when naming your college and degrees are purely optional, with the preference given to words being spelled out. However, if an abbreviation of something (e.g., *Univ.* instead of *University*) prevents you from dropping to the next typewritten line and wasting space, do it. It is extremely doubtful that any employer would discard your résumé because you typed *B.A.* instead of *Bachelor of Arts.*

Odds and Ends: Through the examples shown in the *Education* section, editing techniques have already been provided in most instances when it comes to writing about your college majors/minors, G.P.A., seminars, etc. Basically, you have three options: (1) You may write a sentence about each one, which takes up space; (2) You may itemize them; or (3) You may write a sentence about some and itemize the others. The rule of thumb is probably this: If you want to brag a little more about something, write a sentence about it; otherwise itemize it.

Here is an example of sentences being written:

B.A., Greenwich College, 1933
  — Majored in History, minored in Psychology, and G.P.A.
    was 3.6. Achieved a 3.9 in major. Earned 50% of college expenses in the summer and while working part-time during the school year.

Here is an example of the components being itemized:

Greenwich College   B.A.   1933
- Major: History; Minor: Psychology
- G.P.A.: 3.6 (Major: 3.9)
- Earned 50% of college expenses
- $5000 scholarship from Grimm Foundation

Other Education
- "Creativity," a 3-day seminar
- Subscribe to all the leading historical periodicals
- Read two history books per week

The latter approach is easier to see, but if several additions are made, it becomes a horrible space waster. Before you know it, you can eat up several lines. Nevertheless, for those who do not have that much, it is a good option.

When including the actual names of seminars, be sure to either underline them or surround them with double quotation marks. If, as a new graduate, you are writing about earning your college expenses it is sometimes impressive to state the amount of hours you worked each week during the school year. However, after you enter the working world that fact quickly begins to diminish in importance. In fact, you may not even want to mention it. Make no mention of the dean's list when your G.P.A. is less than a 3.0. As an individual with experience, no mention of the dean's list should be made at all, even if you had a 4.0, for you are no longer writing about your *potential*, but rather your *performance*. Scholarships, like earning your college expenses and having a good G.P.A., should rarely be mentioned in your second résumé, unless they are highly prestigious.

Finally, keep asking yourself: "Am I padding the education section? Would the employer really be interested in that bit of information?" Also, feel free to move things around; underline, capitalize, or indent them, or experiment in any way you wish in order to attain what you consider to be the most effective presentation of information. There is not just one way.

Employment

A description of your current job should be written in present tense. Past jobs, including any you may have held with your present employer before assuming the duties you have now, may be written in present or past tense.

Here are some lead-in words that may be used when you wish to explain your current position.

Accountable for...	Hold the position of (title)...
Activities include...	Involved in...
Activities involve...	In the position of (title)...
Concerned with...	In the role of (title)...
Currently involved in...	Job functions encompass...
Currently engaged in...	Job functions include...
Currently responsible for...	Job functions involve...
Duties encompass...	Presently responsible for...
Duties include...	Responsible for...
Engaged in...	Serve as (title)...

To describe previous jobs the same words may be used, only in the past tense.

Some Tips: Editing the information regarding your work experience should show the employer, in as few words as possible, how your background may benefit him. Never itemize your job duties in a vertical row. While this is often acceptable when writing about your education, it wastes far too much space on the page when used in relation to your employment. It also makes your job seem too clinical, and it makes it especially difficult to highlight anything.

Job Title: You may place your job title directly below the name of the employer, or you may place it in the first line of the information that is below the name of your employer.

Fast Manufacturing Company	*Fast Manufacturing Company*
Title: Production Manager	*As Production Manager for...*

When describing a series of duties, place commas between each.

Responsible for supervising 16 people in the timekeeping department, filing tax returns, developing a weekly plan, and devising controls.

Editing Your Résumé

When grouping your activities, separate the groups with semicolons.

> In the area of FUNDS ADMINISTRATION, ensure that strong controls are maintained over the receipt, custody, and disbursement of the company's assets; in ACCOUNTING, establish policies and standards, implement data processing analyses, and conduct audits; in TAX ADMINISTRATION, direct . . .

Notice that all of the letters of the major components are capitalized. They could have also been underlined or italicized. Whatever approach is selected, your job's major components should be highlighted in some way, to make them stand out on the page; otherwise they will bleed into the rest of the copy and make for harder reading.

Your duties can also follow a colon. If they are single words, separate them with commas. If they are longer, use semicolons.

> Responsibilities were as follows: ensured strong control over company assets; established accounting policies and standards; . . . .

Decide at what length you want to describe your employer, the environment surrounding the job, the responsibilities you handled, what you gained, etc. It remains, as always, a rewriting chore, a case where you compare résumé draft number five with résumé draft number four; and you decide to create résumé draft number six, using a combination of numbers four and five. By doing so, you could wind up with something as brief as this, which states your title, the kind of company it was, and how many customers you had.

> XYZ Company   1976 to 1978
> Performed as a district sales representative for this well-known pharmaceutical company, which required serving 200 accounts.

On the other hand, it could be something more expansive. Here, for instance, the reader learns the job seekers title, work environment, basic responsibility, and what he gained.

Sun Hospital   1981 to 1985

In the position of *Payroll Manager,* serving 3,000 personnel, directed a staff of ten to handle an unceasing heavy work load that included meeting a $100,000 weekly obligation, as well as creating policies that prepared the facility for computer-generated data. Gained an expertise in developing and stream-lining administrative forms, including a keener understanding of a hospital's role in the community.

The Employment "Preface": Imagine you have acquired several years of experience in one field and have worked for three or four employers. Now, while you have gained knowledge and enhanced your own professionalism, earning promotions along the way, you find that while your job duties and working environments have changed over the years, there has not been a dramatic change in going from one to the other. Therefore, you recognize that if you spell out your duties with respect to each employer, there will be a "sameness" between them—a sameness which you may not have felt at all while performing in those jobs, but which is hard to state otherwise on a sheet of paper. You have another option without placing similar information under each employer.

Go through your background and choose those elements which have a sameness from job to job. Write a paragraph that includes *all* of these similar elements. This paragraph is placed below your employment heading, but above your chronological listing of jobs. For example:

<u>Employment</u>

Have acquired more than twelve (12) years of experience in SALES/MARKETING, which has included devising strategies, market analyses, developing...

The Great Company   1981 to Present

As the <u>Marketing Manager</u> for this...

You may also place it under its own heading; in that event, it would be placed *before* the Employment heading. Here are two examples of headings which could be used:

Experience Summary
Synopsis of Background

Regardless of which technique is selected, none of the information in that summarizing paragraph should be repeated in the information beneath each employer.

This paragraph is not only a space saver, but it eliminates a considerable amount of redundancy. This "preface" to your actual employment history provides the employer with an overview of your total background.

To achieve a paragraph of this nature, follow this procedure: look over what you have previously written in relation to each job you have held, to determine the predominant job classification; count the number of companies who have employed you in relation to this activity, including the number of years and the type of companies they were (if important); determine what you believe to be the major functions of your total work experience, as opposed to detailed duties. You may choose subheadings instead, but do not use major headings with them. Then tie it all together.

> Have a 13-year background in MAINTENANCE MANAGE-MENT, in association with four production companies, and major areas of experience include plant engineering, purchasing, budgeting, planning, scheduling, and project planning.

If your experience is not in tune with your objective, it is not a good idea to use the experience synopsis. In that case you would want to downplay such experience as much as possible.

Career Changer: As a career changer, your editing task is boldly clear: refrain from including any job duty that cannot, in some way, relate to the type of career you are seeking. If that means you are only left with a list of the places where you have worked, the dates, and your title while there, then so be it, because including it will certainly not effectively advertise you; in fact, it may well work to your disadvantage when the employer reads it. He can not relate to it.

Usually, the preface to one's employment profile should not be used by the career changer—primarily because there is no applicable experience to draw upon in order to support the objective stated in the first paragraph. Yet, an exception to that general rule would be the occasion when certain bits of experience, which are related to the new objective desired, are attained through past employment. It, too, can be fashioned into a one-paragraph preface that may well help the hiring employer to see that you have some relevant experience. Then, when it comes to listing your various employment periods, you may write as little as one sentence about each. If you have held only one job, however, you must not use the employment preface approach.

New Graduate: The preface approach, explained previously in this section, is often an ideal alternative for the new graduate whose work experience is spotty or, at best, unrelated to what he or she wishes to do. Here, again, the new job hunter must analyze his or her background to find elements to be used.

> As a full-time student, employment has been limited to summer and part-time jobs. During these periods, I have gained some insight into the elements that comprise proper CUSTOMER SERVICE, and I have witnessed the importance of PLANNING and EMPLOYEE RELATIONS.

Similar Jobs: When the difference between the jobs are hard-to-detect, pare the information down to the bone, and make some stand with only one or two sentences rather than duplicating the same information on your résumé. If one job is similar to another that has already been described, say so, and simply note their *differences*. Example:

> Responsibilities were similar to those described under Jerry's Restaurant. However, the customer volume was twice as large.

Concerning any of the jobs you have held, you may well ask yourself if others in the same line of work perform the same duties. And if they do, is there any need for you to include all of yours? Or any of them? If there is no need to list them other than to help fill up your typewritten page, what else can you say that could be more enlightening? What exactly would interest the employer? Does the title, alone, say it all? If it does, perhaps that's all you need.

Eliminating Employers: You may eliminate any employer from your résumé that you wish, unless you take one out of the middle, thereby leaving a gap. Even then you can do it, providing the time you worked there was very brief.

Editing Your Résumé

Suppose you have worked for three employers over a ten-year period. Of them, the second, the WWW Company, was an unfortunate choice, lasting only a few months. You decide to risk not making any mention of it, because you wish to prevent the possibility of your getting a bad reference from someone there who didn't like you. To do this, you drop the months from the employment dates, listing only the years. So, rather than the sequence looking like this:

> The BBB Co. ~~Aug.~~ 1961 to Present
> ~~The WWW Co. May 1961 to Aug. 1961~~
> The ZZZ Corp. ~~Oct.~~ 1955 to ~~May~~ 1961

Now it looks like this:

> The BBB Co.   1961 to Present
> The ZZZ Co.   1955 to 1961

This should only be done when an employment period is relatively brief, and you feel that it is potentially harmful to the overall impact of your résumé, or when you are embarrassed by having worked somewhere. What are they going to do if they catch your omission? Would you have been considered for the job if you had left that one employment period on your résumé?

You may well ask if it is all right to alter the dates of employment, in order to make the potential employer think you worked somewhere longer than you did. This is absolutely not acceptable.

Employment Dates: When the time span at a company was brief, stating the month you started work and the month you left is usually encouraged. However, if you want to hide the fact that your time with an employer was short, stating the years rather than the months makes it appear that you were there longer. When your résumé gets you an interview, and you are asked why you didn't type in the months too, you can be unmercifully blunt by telling the interviewer that you preferred to lose a job because of a bad interview rather than because of a pair of dates on a résumé.

Contrasting Jobs: Wildly contrasting jobs can be a detriment. When you have jobs on your résumé that clash, attempt to eliminate some of the earlier ones, and soften the contrast between those which are left by playing up those aspects they may have in common — if you can find any. Otherwise, to the reader, a patchwork career can be confusing to follow and not worthy of respect.

Achievements

Achievements are described in the past tense, although in some cases they may be preceded by a verb that is in the present tense (see second example, below).

> *Devised* a system whereby....
> After *solving* the problem, *devised* a system....

Editing your achievements is no different from editing any other portion of your résumé. Faced with a certain amount of words and phrases, you merely begin cutting away at them, combining them when necessary or convenient, until you are convinced that you can do no more. The important thing to remember when editing an achievement is that you must never lose sight of its "selling" feature.

Seeing the result first is usually the best, but the other way is quite acceptable. In fact, when you have more than one, you may wish to *begin* one achievement with its result, while with another you may put it at the *end*. Here is where underlining can be particularly important, as long as your résumé does not already have ample underlinings.

- Increased bread and baker sales 21% in three months, by developing a better display method.
- Developed a method to display bread and other bakery items, which increased sales by 21% over three months.

When several achievements are realized during the same employment period and they all lead toward a greater accomplishment, it is sometimes better to calculate the result of them *all* than it is to show individual results and a final result. Making such a decision has a lot to do with how much space you can afford.

- Developed a franchise program that turned a profit in less than three months; upgraded three dealerships that produced a marked change in public attitude; increased efficiency by 75% by having computers installed. Because of these actions the company doubled its profit in one year.

- Doubled the company's profit in one year, by developing a successful franchise program, upgrading three dealerships, and greatly increasing efficiency through computerization.

Always begin an achievement with an action verb, examples of which are shown in the Achievements section (pp. 39–40).

When you are listing more than one achievement, place the most impressive one first, followed by the second best and so forth. It makes no difference if it occurred five years earlier than several others, it still gets top billing. For instance, if you saved the company $850,000 in 1980 and made them $50,000 in 1983, the 1980 achievement gets first mention. Don't tell the employer *when* they occurred. You can do that during the interview.

Regarding the insertion of several achievements, you have two alternatives:

1. Place all of them under their own heading (e.g., "Achievements" or "Accomplishments"), listing them in the order of their importance. For example:

> Achievements
> First achievement
> Second achievement

2. Place them beneath the employer(s) where the achievement happened. For example:

> Last sentence about one period of employment.
> — First Achievement
> — Second Achievement

If you have one achievement, you may wish to include it with the information about the job.

> . . . and analysis of the 35 domestic and foreign reporting units.
> Reduced home office accounting staff by almost 50%.

Sometimes several smaller accomplishments can produce one *major* accomplishment. Suppose you began with these components:

> Developed a stronger distributor network
> + Purchased modern equipment at a 45% savings
> + Negotiated a favorable union contract
> = A 65% profit increase over last year.

You might put the result first and the actions second:

> Increased profit by 65% by developing a stronger distributor network, purchasing equipment at a 45% savings, and negotiating a favorable union contract.

Two or more of your achievements may be combined to make a bold one-sentence statement, which is placed after the very last sentence in your first paragraph. It should not, however, contain specifics, but it should be either underlined or typed in italics, to set it apart from the other information. For example:

> . . . creating repeat business through positive human relations. *Have generated over $12.5 million in sales over the last five years, for two employers.*

You may include as many achievements as you desire on your résumé. They can constitute up to 50 percent of the total work.

After It's Edited

After you have edited your résumé, set it aside for a day or two. Get your mind off it. Then, come back to it. And when you do, try to forget that it is *your* résumé. Instead, put yourself in the shoes of the employer. It's Monday morning. There is a big stack of paperwork facing you, and you dread the thought of going through it. In anticipation of what usually happens when you sift through things like this, you take your foot and drag the trash can closer to you. After tossing most of the résumés away, near the bottom of the stack you come across one that is exactly like yours.

Editing Your Résumé

Now, look at it as if you were seeing it for the first time. Block out all those things you wanted to write, and confine your attention solely to what you have written. As the reader (not the author), ask yourself this question: "What is the writer of this résumé trying to sell?" If it appears to be a direct appeal that is well supported, it is possible that your information is well-edited, for you have gotten the main idea across.

It is essential for you to understand that you are not writing to please some publisher. What you have is merely a one- or two-page résumé that will be sent to people who, without any finely-honed critical abilities, will read what you have written to determine if it is worth their while to have you enter their office for an interview.

Layout and Design

Layout is the order in which the reader views the information you are giving him. Keeping in mind that many employers breeze through a stack of résumés as if each only had one word printed on them, it is important that you do not save your best information till last. Beyond an opening paragraph, where you introduce yourself, the rest of the paper space is ready to be claimed by whichever has the biggest clout.

Design is the final and most critical feature in the whole résumé development process, for if you do not make your information appealing to the eye, your chances of standing out in the crowd are practically nil. The typestyle you choose, the bold printing and graphics used, the size of your headings, the margins and spacing allowed, and the overall quality are a part of design. It enlivens what you worked so hard to create.

The Layout

Given that you should have some type of introductory paragraph, one that states a job objective or a field of interest, here are guidelines which may prove to be helpful:

- If you are a new graduate, it is likely that you are selling your education (and your youth which goes along with it), and it should be placed second. Unrelated employment might be better inserted near the end, just before any mention of miscellaneous information—with the possible exception of a personal work philosophy and any testimonials you have acquired.
- If you are changing careers, information about your skills, traits,

and talents would be more impressive if set apart and placed in a separate paragraph — probably second — to support your objective in the opening paragraph. Normally your employment should be pushed toward the back, unless you can dig some good information out of it and show how it relates to what you now want to do. Your situation is similar to the new graduate's.

- If you are switching jobs in the same career, you are doubtlessly selling your experience; therefore it should be listed second. However, if you have several accomplishments, a better place for them would be after the first paragraph, followed then by your experience. Your education becomes less and less important (in terms of your résumé) as you gain more experience, until it may even be listed last.

- For the person getting out of the military, his or her situation is much like the career changer or new graduate.

Sometimes you are left with information that has no place to go, so you can't use it. To make some things fit that you don't want to lose, you may be forced into combining them with other information and forming a category of your own creation with a unique headline.

Design

Imagine that two résumés are placed on your desk, each reflecting the career of the *same* person, the differences being the name of the person, college, and employers have been changed on one of them. One résumé is very attractive, quite professional-looking; the other is rather plain in virtually all respects. Without knowing these résumés reflected the career of the same person, which of them would get the most respect from you? The attractive one, probably.

The Importance of Design: The "look" of your résumé telegraphs certain preconceived notions to the employer about the writer of the résumé. A classy-looking résumé gets more respect than one which is not. Sure your competitors may be more qualified, but the manner in which you present yourself could well get you in the door first, or at least within the first group of seriously considered candidates. That's all that can be asked of any résumé, which, as we've said, is an advertisement. But it must be *designed* before it can become one. Product designers have regularly understood one unchanging fact: we are attracted to that which is more beautiful. Although a well-designed résumé will certainly not get you an interview with every employer to whom you send it, it makes people pay attention. It gives you the "edge," if there is an edge to be gotten.

The Typing Stage

Never put the typing of your résumé in the hands of amateurs, because the quality of the typing conveys an image of its own. In fact, if the typing is poor, all other design techniques cannot lift your résumé. The quality of the type always has a subtle effect on the reader. For example, give someone two sheets containing identical information, one produced on sophisticated equipment and the other not, and each placed under fake but different company letterheads, the reader will automatically have a far more positive "image" of the company that used the better equipment—even though the same person typed both.

Contracting for the Typing: It is strongly urged that an actual typewriter not be used at all, but rather a computer—specifically one which is hooked up to a laser printer (a dot-matrix printer is not recommended), because you will want the quality of the type to be first class. If you do not have access to one, it means you will have to pay someone else to do it. At this writing, laser copies are as low as 50¢ per page (it may or may not get lower); and a good typist will charge anywhere from $10 to $25 per hour. Do not fail to get a firm price at the very beginning. You don't want surprises. If they refuse to quote a definite, final price, go somewhere else. Your cost will likely depend on the stage of the information you hand over to be reproduced by the computer. If you provide handwritten sheets that are hard to decipher, you may well expect the price to be higher than if you first typed the information on your portable typewriter. The latter is preferable by far, for this reason: you can indicate what you want done by using a coding system of different colored highlighters and passing them over some words and phrases, allowing the typist to quickly understand what you want with regard to underlining, italics, capitalization, bold print, large type, etc. Don't waste the individual's time by going over every detail and expecting him or her to take notes. And should you decide to do that, it would not at all be unfair for him to charge you for the time it took.

Places which are likely to have a computer and laster printer include the following:

Source	Where to Begin Your Search
Quick printers	"Printers" in Yellow Pages
Secretarial services	Business-to-Business Yellow Pages
Desktop publishers	Business-to-Business Yellow Pages
Typing services	Classified section of Sunday newspaper
	Business cards on college bulletin boards

Of these, desktop publishers represent the best source and place to begin.

Make sure you have your résumé produced on equipment whose manufacturer is long-standing. You will want the computer disk which contains your résumé; make that understood at the very beginning. Never leave the office with your résumé without taking along your disk as well. (A disk should only be a few dollars). This way you may take the disk to anyone who owns such equipment and have your résumé changed or reproduced quickly for a very slight fee. Your master is on the computer disk, not on one or two sheets of paper. Wrap the master in plastic and put it away at home.

Essential Options: While you may only use two or three, a computer software program that can produce different sizes of type is necessary. For example:

This is 9 point.
This is 10 point.
This is 12 point.
This is 14 point.
This is 18 point.
This is 24 point.

Layout and Design

It will allow you to quickly make a word stand out on the page.

Seeking a position as a NURSE....

Depending upon what you want to highlight on your résumé, the equipment should be able to provide you with *italics in the middle of a paragraph*. Likewise, it should be capable of **darkening letters** when you want to draw the reader's eye toward an accomplishment.

... established communications with fast-food chains, which ultimately **increased sales by 45% and provided more referrals.**

However, rather than darken a word or phrase, having equipment that can automatically underline as something is being typed would be an advantage, too. Underlining is an equally effective design tool when applied properly.

... established communications with fast-food chains which ultimately <u>increased sales by 45% and provided more referrals.</u>

But with regard to any of the techniques just mentioned, it is essential for you to remember not to overdo it; otherwise it will lose its effectiveness. Too much underlining, word darkening, or italics can make the résumé look "busy." Restrict their use to the important matters.

Right-Hand Justification: Only word processors and the more sophisticated typewriters provide the option of aligning all the words evenly on the right-hand side. It looks nice, but you can easily do without it and the employer won't think worse of you. In fact, many publishers of magazines and books are turning away from right-hand justification as a result of consumer research which has found that people express a preference for typewritten lines that do not end in precise military order.

Typestyles: A word processing program with a variety of typestyles may be important to you, too. No more than two typestyles should be used on any one résumé. Too many different typestyles on a page makes it look as bad as if you had too much underlining or word darkening. Never type a whole résumé in script or italics.

There are literally hundreds of typestyles, but do not expect a typing service to have them all. In fact, you may find no more than a half-dozen at any one place. On the other hand, printers who have invested in computerized equipment to augment their capabilities as well as desktop publishers, will have a great many.

Different typestyles help to enhance the design of a résumé. For instance:

You can use one type for your name	**John Doe**
. . . then a smaller version for headings	**Objective**
Finally, another type for the actual text	Seeking a position as . . .

Those who are engaged in desktop publishing may show you an array of possible choices. Ask to take a look at what they have and listen carefully to their advice; these people often know what is and is not an appropriate typestyle for what you want. Remember, use no more than two. One for your name and headings; the other for the rest of your résumé.

It is also important that you have a good feel for the career which you are in or are pursuing. If, for example, you want a position in a field that is usually populated by people who are conservative (e.g., law, medicine, engineering, accounting, etc.), a name printed like this. . .

Phileas T. Bottom

. . . might certainly be preferable over one like this:

Phileas T. Bottom

But others may find the second alternative a refreshing tonic for the design of their résumés. Know your career field and act accordingly. Or, use one low-keyed typestyle throughout.

Name and Address: Your address should always appear in a regular typestyle, matching that which is used for the body of your résumé. Further, at the top of the page, your name and address may be placed on the left, right, or in the middle. For example:

John Doe
1010 Emerald Street   Cincinnati, Ohio 45213   (513) 631-6787

John Doe
1010 Emerald Street   Cincinnati, Ohio 45213   (513) 631-6787

John Doe
1010 Emerald Street
Cincinnati, Ohio 45213
(513) 631-6787

Your name may even be placed at the bottom right-hand corner, with your address and phone number being in one long, straight line beneath it (a duplicate of the second example, above). In this case, however, your name must definitely be in larger letters, as shown.

Headings: Though your headings are also printed in a larger type, they are never as large as your name. Depending on the size used for your name, they can be one-half the size, or two-thirds at the very most. If your name and address are in the left-hand corner, your headings should follow down the page on the same side. If centered, your headings should be centered down the page. If placed at the upper right or at the bottom right-hand side, your headings are listed on the left-hand side.

You can eliminate your headings altogether. In place of the heading, the first letter of the first sentence is enlarged considerably. For instance:

Design is the cornerstone of my background...

Education includes a B.A. in Art from...

Whitespace: Giving your information room to breathe is a part of design, too. That so-called breathing room is normally termed "whitespace."

On your résumé, whitespace will be blank, and the more effectively it is used on all four sides of the information you present, as well as between the categories, etc., the more professional-looking your résumé will probably look and the better chance you have of making someone read what you have written.

Abuse of White Space: You have perhaps seen some résumés where a heading or employment date is placed on the left-hand side of the page, and all of the other information is crammed into a right-hand column. It is a résumé that is completely unbalanced. The first example shows a date; the second, a heading.

Dec. 1987 to Present:	Information is placed on the right-hand side
Employment History:	Information is placed on the right-hand side

White space is indeed important, but do not waste it all on dates or headings.

Margins: Leave from ¾" to 1" border of white space all the way around your résumé. To gain more white space, do the following:

Left Side:	1¼" from side of page
Right Side:	1¼" from side of page

Spacing: Proper spacing is needed between categories, as well as between the paragraphs within those categories. Some individuals feel obligated to fill the page with words, but all they do is *clutter* it. Do not make the reader's eyes have to crawl through a maze of information. To provide you with some guidelines in this area, here are a few suggestions you may wish to review.

1. Space down four to five lines after your address has been typed.

2. Enter the first heading of your résumé.

3. Space down two lines.

4. Enter your opening paragraph of information.

5. Space down four to five lines after your first paragraph.

6. Space down four to five lines between each category throughout the rest of the résumé.

7. Double or triple space between paragraphs within a category.

8. If you want a certain paragraph to stand out, to feature an achievement or something else you think is important, indent it about 10 spaces from the left margin and precede it with some type of graphic, such as a bullet (•). Structurally, it looks like this:

Paragraph
  •Paragraph
Paragraph

Bullets, Asterisks, Etc.: There are many small graphics that can be used to highlight something you consider important but you should be warned that overuse can clutter your résumé. Therefore, never use more than one kind, and be careful how you use that one. For example, if you indent a paragraph and place a bullet (•) before it, be certain that all subsequent bullets are placed at the same indented space throughout the résumé.

- Information
- Information
- Information

Refrain from using the asterisk (*) before a group of words. Its proper use is to inform the reader that a footnote is at the bottom of the page.

Photographs

Unless you are in the theater or you are in some form of public relations where your appearance is absolutely critical, including a photo of yourself is usually not a good idea. It leaves the door open for the reader to find fault with your appearance. If you believe it will give you the edge in more instances than it doesn't, however, then put it in. Getting that edge is what a résumé is supposed to do.

Never *attach* a photo. It should be printed on the résumé itself. Any other approach is unprofessional. Your local printer can tell you how the printing of photographs on paper works.

It should be placed in the upper right-hand corner. Place your name and address in the left-hand corner, or directly below the picture in smaller letters. If the latter alternative is chosen, move the other information on your résumé up even with the top edge of the photograph.

Other Design Techniques

To learn about other design techniques you will want to refer to the Sample Résumés section of this book.

The design possibilities for your résumé, while not endless, are certainly numerous. An excellent source for generating other design ideas for your résumé can be found in observing advertisements in quality magazines. The art departments of the most well-known ad agencies in the nation put them together, and you can steal a concept here and there.

One way of determining if your résumé has any "design quality" is to tape it up on a wall, take about four or five steps backwards to where you can't read the words, and then look at it. Does it appear crowded? Plain? Off balance? Jumbled? Do the important aspects (e.g., achievements) jump off the page at you? Your answers should tell you if you need to do anything more.

In an employment market crowded with résumés that beg for attention, it would be helpful to remember the plight of the person who must wade through them, most of which are so badly written that he becomes weary before he even begins. A well-designed résumé tells the employer that you care about how you present yourself, that you may be someone special since you took the time to make yours different.

Should you want your résumé to appear without any frills whatsoever, then do it that way. But you should be aware of what is available to you.

Going to Press

You may copy it or have it printed. Whichever, once you have received the master copy of your résumé, you will want to review it for its overall design quality and length, as well as locate any mistakes or typographical errors which are in it.

Proofreading

The typist should not be the last person to proofread the typewritten page. You should have someone proofread the résumé for you; then you should proofread it again yourself.

Spelling: If the résumé is typed on a word processor, chances are the typist will have a built-in spelling correction program. That part, then, becomes fairly routine. If you are paying someone to do this for you, you should find out if that service is extra. Some software programs will not detect duplicate words in a row and grammatical errors. This will be your job. Pay for the work which you had done, and then take your résumé home with you to proofread. Make certain that you have an understanding with the typist that you can bring it back for corrections free of charge. The best way to proofread your résumé for spelling errors is to start at the right-hand side of the page and read each line *backwards.* This forces your eye to rest on each word. Circle any misspelled word.

Grammar: To determine if you have words that are missing, out of context, or appear twice in a row, read the résumé aloud, going from word to word carefully.

Questions Before Printing

Everything seems all right, and you feel there will be no reason to stop payment on the check you gave the typist. Yet, before you rush to have copies printed, review the questions which follow. Perhaps one of them might tell you that you have forgotten something.

Design

From a distance, does my résumé seem attractive?
Is there ample "white space" to prevent a crowded look?
Have I used any graphics to draw attention to something?
Have some words been darkened to highlight something?
Is it necessary to indent certain information to make it stand out?
Are my name and category headings in much larger type?
Are my name and headings in proper alignment?
Do my achievements stand out?
Do the *results* of my achievements stand out?
Are my achievements in the order of their importance?
Is my education listed in the order of its importance?
Can the main feature of my background be seen easily?

Categories

Are the categories in the order of their importance?
Should my skills be in a category by themselves?
Should I put my achievements in a category by themselves?
Could any of the categories be combined and made more effective?
Is my testimonial well-placed?

Content

Will the employer have a clear idea of what I want?
Have I stated the total years of experience I have in my field? Or should I?

Have I listed any of the main features of my background? Should I?
Do the personal traits that I have included promote me?
Do my natural talents complement my objective?
Do my skills complement my objective?
Have I said too much about my job duties? Or too little?
Have I painted a good picture of my working environment?
Have I said what I learned at each job?
Are the duties under each job described in the order of their importance?
Could anything in my résumé be a detriment?
Do my school activities help my résumé at all?
Is my grade point average important enough to include?
Do my hobbies, interests, or memberships help my chances?
Does the testimonial I'm using act as a "plus" on my résumé?
Does my personal work philosophy sound trite?
Does my work philosophy match my past performance and objective?
Do I know what I'm advertising? If so, am I doing it?
Do I like the résumés of others' better than mine? If so, why?

Length

On the second page of a two-page résumé, type your name in the top right or center, (using larger lettering if you prefer, but only slightly larger than the rest of the text), and type the page number alongside it. For example:

John Doe—Page Two
John Doe—Page 2

A three-page résumé is never warranted, no matter how impressive you believe your background to be. To send an employer a three-pager means that you have not done proper editing, and that will likewise mean it will probably not be read properly.

There is one exception to that, and it usually applies to that person who is at the managerial level. He or she has a background that is somewhat distinguished as a result of past accomplishments, and the career is not in any of the scientific areas.

Basically, it is still just a two-page résumé; but the information is printed on a sheet of high quality paper that measures 11″ × 17″. When that sheet is folded in half, you have two 8½″ × 11″ sheets facing each other like pages in a book. Using this approach, your name only appears once, and it is centered—in large letters—on the front page which the reader first sees. If a three or four line introduction to the résumé is used, it is placed below the name. However, this space is normally reserved for the address. An example of one type of information that could be used, is as follows:

John Doe

Presenting the career of a manager with fifteen years experience in the field of manufacturing, highlighted by accomplishments and skills.

You have to mail it in a large white or manilla envelope, which allows the résumé to lay flat. This will cost you more postage (even though it is the same weight, because the size changes the rules) as well as more money in envelopes. But it can be well worth it.

Duplicating Your Résumé

As stated before, you have two choices: use either a quick-printer or a copying machine.

The Copy Machine: Going the copying machine route allows you great flexibility, since you are able to duplicate your master copy once or many times. Getting a copy that is absolutely straight on the copy paper can be frustrating. Frequently, the alignment is a bit off because you have not placed your original exactly straight on the glass.

If you are seeking a high-level management position, then your "package" should be top drawer all the way, involving matching envelopes and paper that feels expensive to the touch. You shouldn't use a copy machine for your résumé. The employer handles so many résumés that his discernment of quality or alignment is practically negligible. It definitely won't stop you from being hired if you have the credentials the job requires. Its appearance could gain in importance when the boss is deciding who to invite for an interview, and he places your résumé alongside another which may be straight.

You *can* buy a better grade and texture of paper at an office supply shop and insert it into the paper tray of most copying equipment. You do not have to settle for what is in the machine. Over the past several years there have been some shops that have devoted themselves entirely to producing copies for consumers utilizing very large, high-speed, top-of-the-line equipment. These shops are capable of reproducing your master copy at very reasonable rates (e.g., 5¢ each), and the quality of the work they deliver easily rivals those of the quick printers.

The Quick Printer: Unlike the copying house, the quick printer usually has a policy of printing no fewer than 25 copies. Many times, depending upon whose services you use, it is often cheaper to buy an extra 75 copies, since the difference in price is so slight. The cost is not in the paper, but rather in the labor. You will rarely get bad results from a quick printer. Using an offset press, he provides consistently high quality.

Paper: Expensive paper in the most attractive color cannot make a badly prepared résumé look any better. Only *content* and *design* can do that. Quick printers and copying services are not magicians; they are only as good as what you give them, so don't believe that the type of paper you use will somehow sway the employer. It won't. Consider using a light-grey or a pale-beige type. Black and white are at the opposite ends of the color spectrum; therefore they are not as naturally pleasing to the eye as one would think. Black on grey not only mutes that contrast, but it gives the page an air of distinction as well. Nevertheless, black ink on white paper is still quite acceptable—even expected.

Matching envelopes are not important. The employer often doesn't even see the envelope, his secretary having already removed its contents and either thrown the envelope away or stapled it to the back of the résumé. Still, as a professional who is out there pitching his or her credentials in the job market, if you feel more comfortable with matching envelopes, then get them. This should be particularly true when you are closing in on the higher end of the pay scale. Not only can you afford it, but there is a chance that the secretary will *not* open the envelope; and in that case a plain white envelope and a résumé on colored paper might muddy your professionalism a bit.

Mistakes After Printing: Suppose you print you résumé and later find a mistake. The only thing that is close to being unforgivable is having your name or address typed incorrectly. Dates are a distant second. Once you have paid to have your résumés printed, and you later discover a small error, don't throw them away and have more printed. Use them. No sensible employer is going to discard your résumé if it is otherwise done well and you have the preliminary qualifications. During the interview, should an employer happen to remark about a typographical error he has caught, reply with something like, "That's incredible. I'll bet ten people, including myself, have proofread that résumé, but you're the only one who's caught that. Thanks a lot for telling me. I'm going to get it fixed right away!" You've just made him feel special because he thinks he is the only one who caught the mistake. Little does he know that you were already aware of it.

Employers do not hire people based upon the lack of errors found in their résumés; they normally choose them because of their potential worth to the company.

Sample Résumés

What you will see in this section are a few of the layout and design alternatives available to you. Most of these résumés are not plain, and they may well tend to widen the eyes of those who are used to seeing dull, unimaginative typewritten styles. If you are in a conservative career field (engineering, accounting, etc.), your possible apprehension will be understandable; in fact, some designs would have to be toned down considerably before you could use them. Only first-page examples are being offered here.

Spend very little time, if any, reading what each has to say. Rather, look at them as mannequins in a store window which have yet to be dressed. The borders, the spacing, the placements of one's name and headings — these are the starting points. The words you have written about your own job objective, your past employment, and your education, etc., are the clothes that will adorn them. Avoid any attempt to make your information read like what you see on any of these résumés. Be reminded that you are only limited by your imagination and your courage to be different.

Finally, it is absolutely essential for you to understand that almost all things which have been written could have been done better, and these résumés are certainly no exception. Remember that when you are in the depths of your creative frustration.

Stanford M. Tremont

1231 Williams Street   Louisville, Kentucky 42069   (502) 555-1212

Introduction

Have served as a high-volume producer of sales for a nationally known manufacturer of consumer products over the past five years, covering a four-state territory, and was an award-winning sales representative prior to present employment. Moreover, through formal education and witnessing the techniques practiced in the sales field, I have steadily prepared myself for my next career move, which is to assume the position of...

Sales Manager

...for another organization, though not necessarily in the same product field. Have acquired a solid knowledge of those habits peculiar to buyers and what motivates them to purchase products, as well as how to generate new customers and develop repeat business through positive human relations. I am eager to share this information with other sales professionals, and would be willing to relocate to another geographical area for the right career opportunity.

Education

University of Iowa

- Received a Bachelor of Science in Business Administration, 1971

- Awarded the prestigious Gold Duck Scholarship...elected as Senior Class President...and employed thirty (30) hours per week while attending school. Graduated with a 3.1 G.P.A.

Currently working toward an M.B.A. at the University of Louisville, with concentration of studies in the field of management. Have also completed numerous seminars and company courses in the same area.

Experience

☐   JACOB SPORTING GOODS, 1985 to Present

As a Senior Sales Representative for this well-known company, handle a four-state area that now produces $4.5 million in sales.

- Have increased sales by twenty-five percent (25%) during the last year, and projections indicate at least a twenty percent (20%) rise this year.

Besides interacting with buyers within large retail facilities on a regular basis, position demands extensive

Thomas Wall

138 Picadilly Square   St. Petersburg, Florida 67171   (813) 528-6670

Seeking a position as an **ARCHITECT** with a highly respected firm, particularly one whose efforts are centered upon the development of urban and commercial structures. Possess superior design and drafting skills. Portfolio available upon request.

Received a **Bachelor of Architecture** from the University of Florida in 1980, a six-year stint which involved participation in the highly proclaimed "Professional Practice Program." On a quarterly basis, this required alternating between college classes and on-the-job training, an experience that proved to be dramatically helpful.

After graduating from college, became associated with **Hodell, Baxter, and Preston**—recognized as one of the three leading architectural firms in the St. Petersburg area. Since that time, have been assigned to three (3) major projects. These include the following:

- [ ] a **$50M project** for Procter and Gamble, involving two office buildings, a large laboratory, a pilot building, and a packaging building. Besides being engaged in developing new architectural concepts, directed two (2) co-op students in the completion of drawings for the pilot and packaging structures.

- [ ] a **300,000 square foot office building** for the U.S. Shoe Corporation, which demanded the development of the plan and section details, site and floor plans, and the elevations, as well as participating in many design decisions throughout the production of the final working drawings.

- [ ] a **fifth-floor addition to the headquarters building** of the Houston Oil Company, with duties similar to those described above. Received a letter of accommodation, which said in part, "...*the accuracy and thoroughness of the drawings were outstanding and needed*

Josie Freeman
26 Puff St. Flat, CA 90168   (714) 555-1212

Introduction

Background encompasses virtually all areas of production, layout, logo development, typography, and marker indication. Skilled at conceiving unique and marketable ideas, handling intricate artwork, developing headlines, and operating a Phototypositer and Pos Stat camera. Perform exceptionally well under pressure situations.

While self-employment has several attractive features, the primary one being perhaps the satisfaction of knowing that you are "making it on your own," I miss the camaraderie and the exchange of creative ideas which can be found in a larger staff. Therefore, I have chosen to no longer free lance.

Education

Received a **Bachelor of Arts** (Fine Arts) from Texas University in 1977.

Completed a 2-year intensive art study program at the Thornton Academy of Commercial Art in 1982.

Studied architecture, advanced drawing, and ceramics at Ohio State University in 1980.

Experience

Successfully self-employed, working under the name of **FREEMAN'S FREE LANCE.** Provide paste-ups, keyline, general design, and illustration. The quality of my work has generated excellent word-of-mouth advertising, and have steadily received referrals. However, prefer to create rather than operate a business.

Created a new image for a sports complex by developing a new logo.

Illustrated a mechanical product for a magazine layout, which produced heavy sales for the manufacturer.

From 1981 to 1986, employed by the **SHOP FOR WOMEN.** Created, maintained, and coordinated sophisticated displays and interiors for all seven stores of this retail chain.

Accelerated sales by developing a humorous and much talked-about mannequin display. And because of natural talents in this area, was chosen to instruct two co-op students in attaining esthetically pleasing and balanced window displays.

Ralph G. Simpson

Objective

As a recent graduate in the field of **REAL ESTATE**, desire to secure a position with a quality company which can challenge my interests and provide a rewarding future—more particularly, a company which buys investment properties and needs a professional to perform a wide range of duties, ranging from general research and property evaluation to the actual closing of a deal and the subsequent coordination of repairs, rentals, etc. Have gained meaningful, first-hand experience in this field over the past few years and can offer an employer more than knowledge from books. Now preparing to acquire an MAI designation.

Personal Profile

I am not a 9 to 5 worker; often work long into the night to solve a problem or provide a needed service. Enjoy learning about the "art of making the deal"; and beyond classroom assignments, have read countless books regarding real estate, psychology, sales, and management—a practice I will continue.

Educational Background

University of Tennessee

- Received a B.S.B.A. in Finance, 1983.

- Concentration was in the field of **Real Estate and Urban Development** (e.g., urban economics, portfolio analysis, statistics, property appraisal, etc.).

- Graduated with high honors, attaining a 4.0 G.P.A. in real estate courses and an overall G.P.A. of 3.4.

Employment

J. D. SIMPSON REALTORS

Since 1979, have acquired a background in several aspects of real estate appraisal while in association with this family-owned business. Activities have included, for example, measuring and photographing properties—including drawing them and writing their descriptions—assembling data on comparable properties in the same area, conducting courthouse research, and performing other duties that lead to an effective property analysis.

Additional Information

Have played a contributory role in several areas, all of which have demanded positive human relations.

For instance, served as a Student Coordinator at the Columbus Home—an emergency shelter for abused and abandoned children—during my junior and senior years; previously acted as a volunteer for two years. Was one of three people who actually originated this group, which included recruiting other volunteers and scheduling their assistance. Invited to speak at the Department of Human Resources Convention (1983).

To assist the homeless, initiated a Christmas season program that demanded the supervision of ten personnel. Rented the office space, marketed the concept to business firms, and sold products to consumers—the profits of which were turned over to provide better housing and supply food. Profits grew from $7,000 the first year to more than $15,000 after the second.

3105 Parson Gardens   Memphis, Tennessee 56812   (915) 888-9419

91

Introduction

Possess extensive experience in the area of group insurance, and interested in applying this knowledge toward a position as **Manager of an Employee Benefits Program.** Would be receptive to joining an insurance carrier, a brokerage house, a corporation that needs a highly qualified professional to provide operational leadership in this area, or a similar employer where my skills and experience can be fully utilized.

Strengths and Characteristics

Especially adept at selling, managing, and servicing group insurance and pension programs. Have handled large, multi-division accounts and those which are small, working under the philosophy that no account is so small that it cannot be given the attention it deserves. Skilled at probing and identifying—as well as quickly responding to—the needs of clients, the result being that far fewer problems occur down the line and customer satisfaction, including their loyalty, is maintained. Because of my experience and knowledge of employee benefits, have been quite successful in motivating current clients and new prospects to consider alternate ideas and recommendations, in order to meet my company's sales objectives without sacrificing the needs of the customer.

Considered to be a competitive, conscientious, and patient professional. I produce long-term, beneficial results rather than "quick fixes."

Experience

Ajax Insurance
September 1979 to Present

For the past four years have held the position of <u>Assistant Manager of Group Sales</u> at the Midwest Division of this nationally known insurance firm, and coordinate accounts that range from $500,000 to $15M, involving no less than 200 employees each. Assist the department manager in setting objectives for ninety-five (95) sales professionals, as well as administering more than two thousand established accounts in our division alone. Briefly, my position demands the following: keen attention to detail; handling problems from members of our staff and those received from clients through the mail and over the phone; assigning work to a large clerical staff; devising forms that will improve efficiency; and assuming the duties of the manager in his absence.

Vera B. Tabon

2894 Baker Avenue   Cincinnati, Ohio 45213   (513) 391-3301

B. "Fanny" Williams

4928 Shakespeare Road
Boston, MA 10020
(617) 555-1212

Tennis Instructor

Nine years of experience with top-rated clubs. Have exceptional teaching skills, and recognized for being enthusiastic and imaginative. Career is marked by superb training at the hands of Steve Shadrack, John Whittier, and Tim Wrath; and have acquired an excellent reputation for working with the state's top junior tournament players. Seeking a position as Tennis Instructor for an organization located in the southwestern part of the United States.

Career Credentials

Generating Profit   Able to help increase the profit of an athletic facility through the following methods: creating positive camp environments (have supervised up to 10 personnel and coordinated 50 players weekly); providing private lessons that have proven to be quite motivational and which produce superb results; and organizing tennis parties, round-robins, league play, tournaments, and special events, all of which have established good public relations and have brought in new memberships (average 25% new members yearly).

Employment   Previously acted as the tennis professional for Willow Grove Country Club (1979-1983), and now serving in the same capacity for the East Side Racquet Club (1983 to Present). Was a part-time instructor for the Angel Sports Center between 1975 to 1977. *My students have a high rate of victory regarding tournament matches.*

Languages   Can speak Spanish and French fluently, and have a light command of German. Spent ten (10) weeks traveling throughout South America. Unanimously chosen to supervise a select group of members from various clubs in the Boston area regarding a two-week tennis club circuit in France, in 1985.

Education   Bachelor of Physical Education, University of Canton, 1977.

     • Graduated with a 3.3 G.P.A.

Other Information   Winner of the Pennsylvania Singles Title in 1977.

NELSON CHADWICK
Manufacturing Engineer

Introduction

Presenting a career which encompasses strong experience in the areas of **Maintenance , Facilities, and Plant Engineering,** and have also been heavily involved in computer-controlled manufacturing operations. Exceptionally skilled at planning/scheduling, cost reduction, key decision-making, problem-solving, and project control and coordination. Currently searching the job market to determine if a position is available that will challenge my abilities and offer an opportunity to increase my own career expertise.

Experience

☐   Tri-Motor Manufacturing Company—September 1983 to Present

As the <u>Assistant Manager of Manufacturing Engineering</u> within the Trim and Chassis plant of one of the world's most technologically advanced facilities, responsible for three (3) maintenance shifts, two (2) product lines, and a $3M budget. Accountable for over 9 miles of overhead conveyor...2 miles of floor conveyor...and process equipment (among which includes automatic tire and wheel assembly units, Dominion evacuation and fill equipment, Burke & Porter tester equipment, micro-poise alignment machinery, and robots that automatically selects tires and apply anti-rust wax).

All of this equipment is controlled by computer, microcomputer, or microprocessor (i.e., Hitachi HIDAC-80; NESP-R controllers and 2-E's; DEC 2450; Micro-84's, 484's, and 584's; and Allen Bradley PLC 2-20's).

Currently working on a system that will apply butyl rubber to windshield assemblies via robot. Besides consistently maintaining less than one-half of a percent downtime in a plant of this complexity and size, have also played a major role in the following activities (achievements):

The design of an Integrated Maintenance Management System, which accumulates data for better cost analysis, trend-setting, maintenance planning regarding equipment.

The design of a broad-based, fiber-optics, high speed communications system to handle fire protection, energy use, plant environment, and computer "conversation." Work order permits are automatically printed out.

| 1414 McCormick Dr. | St. Louis, MO 61911 | (314) 216-2121 |

Hillary J. Miller

3505 Waycross Street, Columbus, OH. 44186, (614) 721-8891

Career Objective

As a 1985 graduate with a degree in zoology, wish to formally launch my career by securing a position as a **MARINE MAMMAL TRAINER**. Have already acquired valuable experience as an apprentice dolphin trainer during the past two summer seasons. For example, have observed and assisted in dolphin training, participated in show performances, prepared their food, handled stadium and prop maintenance chores, cleaned equipment, and, importantly, have taught children about dolphins.

Educational Profile

Ohio State University

— Bachelor of Science, Zoology, 1985.
— Maintained a 3.8 G.P.A. while working 25 hours weekly.
— Earned 50 percent of college expenses.
— Vice President of senior class.
— Member of varsity team in swimming, soccer, basketball, and softball; captain of the swim and soccer teams in junior and senior year.

Employment

TAMPA BAY MARINE WORLD, Summers of 1983 and 1984

Assisted the director in a wide range of activities, the most important of which have been listed above. In addition, gained valuable knowledge in office procedures, federal and state forms, budgeting, and most especially how to put on an entertaining marine show.

WIGGIN'S DEPARTMENT STORE, 1982 to 1985

On a part-time basis, worked evenings and weekends as a sales clerk, cashier, and shipping clerk, as well as three wonderful stints as the store's Easter Bunny.

Designer...

of brochures, print advertisements, annual reports, packaging, letterheads, catalogues, invitations, books and manuals, self-mailers, etc., with more than ten years of experience and a comprehensive knowledge of all design phases up to and including the final printing of projects that use multiple colors. For advertising accounts, quite adept at isolating—through research and interviews—the specific marketing problem regarding a product or service and marrying the client's view of it with the needs in the marketplace, using bold concepts that generate responses.

Would be interested in discussing possible employment with a firm who needs an "idea person"; one who can readily establish themes and images; one who is conscientious, analytical, and creative.

Accomplishments...

have been varied and numerous, not limited to any one area. Three examples follow.

Created a logo for one client that not only changed the theme of the company's advertising programs substantially, but it became highly recognizable and popular among the public, the result being that sales experienced a steady climb because of product recognition.

For a publisher, handled a how-to book project that had generated disappointing sales. Selected what I considered to be the essential selling feature—one that had been surprisingly overlooked— and highlighted it by redesigning the cover and providing illustrations at the head of each chapter, giving them more drama and a sense of urgency. The publisher sold ten thousand copies during the first month of the book's re-issue.

Developed a two-color brochure for a new membership club, which the officers say was instrumental in increasing their membership by 40 percent.

Employment ...

since January 1986 has been with TIFTON'S. Originally hired as a Layout Artist and Hard-Line Illustrator for this well-respected, growing organization, but I have since been promoted to **ASSISTANT LEAD DESIGNER** because of my continuing contributions to the company's success. Moreover, I assume the duties of the Lead Designer in his absence, something which occurs with more than the usual frequency.

Previously self-employed (1983 to 1986) and gained considerable sales expertise and human relations skills while earning a living in the competitive field of design. Besides being a free lance artist and sharpening my artistic skills during this period, also acquired a strong appreciation of what it takes to run a business (buying, administration, planning, scheduling, etc.).

Holly Clark

Holly Clark   1215 Ridge Road   Chicago, IL 52215   (312) 729-0799

Sarah Miles

Objective

Seeking a position as an **Administrative Assistant.** Possess several years of experience in helping a high-level executive organize and maintain an efficiently-run office. With a background in data processing, customer relations, purchasing, and organizing business and social functions, wish to become associated with a take-charge individual who needs a can-do assistant. Although I have thus far been employed by firms in the beauty products field, have the skills and knowledge to easily adapt to any type of organization. Prefer a company which is aggressive in the marketplace, and particularly want an environment which is fast-paced and demands decision-making. Basically, I wish to make a contribution; if I can't, the job is not worth doing.

Skills and Traits

Have superior organizational ability, and my memory is well above average. Human relations skills are exceptional; moreover, I fully understand the chasm that often exists between management and employees within a company, and I usually serve as a buffer and liaison to improve communications and prevent any misunderstanding between them. Recognized as an outstanding typist with a strong knowledge of grammar and punctuation; and viewed by others as being efficient and positive-thinking. I'm the person they run to when those thorny little problems crop up from out of nowhere.

Experience Synopsis

Have served as an Administrative Assistant for two leading cosmetic firms—one in New York and the other in Chicago—leaving only to raise a family. During that time, I gained considerable knowledge of what it takes to "make things easier on the boss," and was credited with several achievements that were beneficial to my employers. For example:

EXQUIS, INC.   Acting on my suggestion regarding shipments to wholesalers, Exquis reduced its costs by 20%, and tighter controls were implemented. Also initiated the purchase of a phone system that greatly improved communications with the company's clientele as well as between individuals within the company itself.

BAISER   On my own, analyzed invoices over a year's period and discovered the company was being overcharged 15%. Nearly a hundred thousand dollars was refunded.

8514 Windcrest Drive   Chicago, Illinois 50966   (312) 555-1212

97

Beverly C. Johnson

451 Meir Lane, Cleveland, Ohio 44922, (216) 555-1212

Health Promoter and Educator. Interested in assuming a similar position with an organization in the New England area, where extensive knowledge may be applied to reduce spiraling medical costs and increased absenteeism, which ultimately affect profit. As a professional who believes—and has consistently proven—that lifestyle and self-image are the major factors which affect one's health, have authored, planned, designed, and presented health programs that are effective.

Summary of experience over the past ten years begins with my personal goal: to heighten the health awareness of employees and encourage their participation on a day in-day out basis. An overview of activities since entering this challenging field includes the following:

- Establish contact with decision-makers throughout the community, to generate an interest in helping others.

- Manage clinics to assist individuals in handling stress, improve their nutrition and physical conditioning, stop smoking, and learn how to live a purposeful and full life.

As my programs have shown to work, have been quite successful in raising morale (meanwhile, production within the organization has increased as well); and I have documented the results, later presenting them in a book I authored, entitled the *Spirit Wellness Manual*.

Education includes both a MASTER OF ARTS and a BACHELOR OF ARTS, received in the years 1972 and 1980 from The Athenaeum of Ohio. Majored in Health Administration and minored in Physical Education.

Health Director for the Times Company since 1979, and have been responsible for developing, promoting, and presenting in-house health workshops. This requires, for example, simplifying and systemizing the available information and arranging it so that it may be presented effectively in both written and oral form; motivating others to work cooperatively and giving them recognition for their accomplishments; supervising a staff of seven (7) personnel; and handling an assortment of administrative tasks, among which includes budgeting and policy definitions.

- During this time, have been a guest speaker on radio talk shows—namely WVIK and WGUT in Cleveland.

Leslie L. Reckers

1486 Paxton Avenue, Apt. 21
Denver, Colorado 78122
(303) 555-1212

Objective

Seeking a position in **FOOD SERVICE**, preferably as an assistant to the chef, where I can use my education and further add to my experience in the culinary arts.

Credentials

My education and part-time employment represents my primary background in this field which I have chosen as my career. Specifically:

Education

Will graduate from the renowned **Cordon Bleu School of Cookery** in May 1982, finishing in the top 5 percent of my class. Here I have learned the rudiments of preparing Cajun meals, in addition to the traditional French, Italian, and Oriental cuisine. As part of Cordon's program, have served as **Chef's Assistant** at three separate locations in the city, each lasting a week.

Prior to the above, attended Colorado University for two years and majored in **Business Management**. Need only four credit hours to receive an Associate Degree. Planning, scheduling, budgeting, and purchasing were among the areas studied.

Experience

Have worked in my family's **catering** business since the age of sixteen, helping my father prepare salads and vegetables—almost everything, in fact, except the main entrées. Gained considerable knowledge about how to: plan for small and large groups; arrange food on a table to make it appear most appealing; and run a business.

While working in the catering business and later at Cordon, have proven that I can perform well under severe time limitations; that I am quick, physically and mentally; and that I have above-average organizational and human relations skills. Possess an inner competitiveness; for not only am I the kind of person who insists on doing my job right, but I enjoy doing it better than I did the day before.

Thomas H. McCormick

1705 West Kiles Avenue
Yukon, Idaho 80019
(901) 555-1212
Business 661-5555
(Free to talk at work)

Introduction

Desire to join the Advertising Sales staff of a major eastern metropolitan newspaper. Have ten (10) years experience in this field, and I have increased sales every year. Here are two comments from my employers:

> "He joined our staff during a time of sagging sales. As a result of developing new ideas—particularly his concept concerning the 'Pick-Up Ad Program' that we adopted—our sales turned around, and we realized a 20% upturn within months. We will miss him if he leaves our organization." —Benjamin Burner, Owner, *The Yukon.*

> "Any newspaper that needs a salesman who knows how to generate new sales and keep the customers already on board, I would strongly advise them to get in touch with Tom McCormick. He is unquestionably the best."—Ted Drury, Owner, *The Woodlawn Weekly.*

Experience

The Yukon

Accepted the position of Sales Representative for this paper because its sagging sales offered a great challenge and I was given the opportunity to communicate with national accounts. Besides developing the Pick-Up Ad Program, which turned the *Yukon's* art department into a vital sales force itself and significantly moved the customer's "wants" closer to his actual "needs," launched an all-out campaign to secure advertising in areas that had not previously been considered. Developed a "cooperative" advertising program for the sports and business pages that was readily accepted by those advertisers who had yet to use the newspaper. **As a result of these efforts, sales steadily increased and the paper's base of advertisers was strengthened and widened.** Subsequently promoted to Senior Sales Representative.

Woodlawn Weekly

In addition to securing new business as a Sales Representative, provided customers with advertising advice and developed new ways to promote their products or services. This often required problem-solving, performing ad layouts, and directing the dispersal of

100

Wilma Feffner

3841 Moorehouse Lane, Miami,Florida 35992, (305) 667-8521

Career Objective

Having earned my bachelor's degree, now wish to apply this knowledge—as well as my practical experience—toward a rewarding position in a **BUSINESS** environment. Interests at this time are wide, but seek a position that will provide an opportunity to gain considerable knowledge. Particularly want to become associated with an employer who encourages the development of new ideas and who will act on those which, after careful analysis, appear worthy of pursuing.

Education

Received a **Bachelor of Business Administration** degree from Florida College, June 1988.

— Attained a 3.7 G.P.A., but it was 4.0 in all business-related courses.

— President of the Profit and Loss Club (See "Experience").

— Subscribed to Forbes, Fortune, Business Week, and the Wall Street Journal, in addition to handling a heavy course load, working part-time, and participating in intramural sports.

At George Washington High School (Carlton, Mississippi), graduated at the top of my class in 1984. As a result, received a $20,000 scholarship from the Carlton Chamber of Commerce.

Experience

FLORIDA COLLEGE

From 1986 to 1988, was part of a three-person project team that assumed the responsibility of **making major changes in a well-known accounts receivable system.** Through research, analysis, and trial and error, we were able to convert the model to a highly efficient data processing system that eliminated most of the tedious paperwork, increased accuracy by 100%, and quickly identified bad credit risks.

Served as **President of the Profit and Loss Club for two years.** Began by implementing a recruitment drive that increased membership from 200 members to more than 500. The requirements of operating this on-campus organization were the same as

Shirley K. Anderson
1789 Westwood Boulevard
Pittsburgh, PA 39921
(412) 555-1212

Introduction

Presenting an extensive background in ENVIRONMENTAL ENGINEERING, specifically in the area of wastewater and solid waste for over twenty (20) production facilities, which produce a variety of products.

Engineering experience includes process development, project engineering for a new manufacturing site, and on-going technical services in relation to existing plants.

Education

University of Pittsburgh   B.S.C.E.   1974

Engineering Experience

☐ THE BAR & POWDER SOAP COMPANY, 1976 to Present
☐ Environmental Engineer

Within a group of remarkably dedicated and talented engineers, help to ensure that this company's numerous production facilities comply with local, state, and federal laws and regulations, as well as the company's own stringent demands. In addition to implementing our engineering expertise to detect and solve problems, it is equally important that we cultivate positive human relations when interacting with all departments, to prevent misunderstanding and finger-pointing.

Besides engaging in such activities as working closely with Research and Development to establish environmental data bases for new and existing products, optimizing designs, submitting permits (e.g., tax relief and discharge types), and instructing engineering and manufacturing personnel in the areas of environmental policies, systems, and plans, have been privileged to play a significant role in the following:

√ The design of the award-winning Philly Plant, which achieved zero sulphur emissions.

√ The creation of the revolutionary XT-75 Software Program, which has proven to provide up-

Sample Résumés

Gregory M. Farris

5317 East Court Street, Apartment 3, Atlanta, Georgia 64166, (404) 541-7878

Professional Objective and Career Profile

OBJECTIVE ...is to secure a position as an HVAC Systems Designer, specifically with a large engineering firm, where my knowledge of complete systems for major construction projects may be effectively used. Have designed systems for office buildings, warehouses, shop areas, cooling for process applications, restaurants, retail facilities, computer rooms, and residential homes.

KNOWLEDGEABLE ...in the following: constant air volume systems; make-up air units; filtration devices; hot water boilers; split systems; infra-red heating systems; dual duct systems; air-to-air heat exchangers; unitary systems in computer rooms; self-contained units; forced air furnaces; and control systems. Experienced in head-load calculations, duct work, piping, equipment, drafting, cost factors, and final installation. Moreover, have consistently kept up to date regarding the new aspects of systems design.

STRENGTHS ...include troubleshooting new or existing systems in commercial and industrial projects with more ease than most professionals in my field. Also able to look at the drawings of a proposed HVAC installation and pinpoint immediate and long-range problems. (I have yet to be proven wrong.) Have a natural design ability, combining my own techniques with those which I have learned about through study and first-hand observation. Possess a meticulous approach to design, in order to get it right the first time and not allow any "fudge factor" to occur.

EDUCATION ...includes an Associate Degree in Mechanical Engineering from Mohawk College (1985). Earned degree while working 40+ hours per week and raising a family. Graduated within the top 10% of my class. Currently enrolled at Tomahawk University, and expect to achieve a B.S.M.E. in 1990.

EMPLOYMENT ...since January 1975 has been with MECHANICAL SYSTEMS, where I serve as a Design Assistant with the Commercial Systems Group. I have been involved in designing infra-red heating systems for several manufacturers. Position requires working within tight deadlines and strict budget restraints. Make on-site inspections, and communicate with the customer's engineers to ensure that what is being done will meet with their approval; this has eliminated misunderstanding and redesign, to a large measure.

From October 1971 to January 1975, employed by SUPERIOR DESIGN, a small company that specialized in producing designs for filtration devices. Besides duties as a Draftsman, was tutored in design by the owner of the operation, who had once been one of the industry's leading designers. During this time, for example, I learned

Harry B. Swan

6603 Waycross Drive
Philadelphia, PA 29966
(215) 631-8831

Objective

Pursuing a position in **DEPARTMENT STORE MANAGEMENT**, specifically with a major department store which enjoys a good reputation in the community. Possess excellent skills in the area of planning, problem-solving (economic, personnel, marketing, etc.), quickly defining trends, and budgeting. Able to offer an employer more than twenty years in the field, ten of which have been in top-level management.

Achievements

Achievements have come as a result of an ability to perform creative merchandising, establish and maintain strong inventory control policies and procedures, develop positive customer service programs, and motivate assistant managers (as well as an office staff) to perform at their best. Among the more notable achievements include the following:

    For my present employer...
        assumed control of a downtown operation that had been losing money over a 2-year period, and (1) through judicious restaffing, (2) significantly reducing the heavy inventory of goods that had poor marketability, and (3) implementing programs via radio and television to change the image of the store, **produced a 21 percent gross profit**—a remarkable improvement compared to the situation when I took over.

    While with my former employer...
        was assigned to a troubled retail facility in Memphis that was close to being shut down. Planned and implemented unique programs in virtually all departments; established "theme weeks," contests for customers, and an low-cost professional photography and video policy; and got the jump on other stores in the area by identifying and quickly marketing a product trend. As a result, **the store experienced a complete turnaround and competed successfully with the other leading retail firms in the city.**

Sample Résumés

lexander K. Frederick

| 1931 Fairfax Road | Thomasville, Kentucky 49921 | (606) 555-1212 |

Introduction

Presenting a background in <u>Financial Management</u> that covers more than fifteen years of experience, all with prestigious organizations. Knowledge comprises management systems analysis, credit, cost control, budget development, taxes, internal auditing, and computer science.

Exceptionally skillful in the following areas: planning and scheduling projects with respect to priorities, people, and time needed; developing computer programs that promote efficiency; streamlining departments; selecting and promoting productive employees who enjoy making contributions to the company; and devising long-range policies and procedures.

Would be interested in meeting with an employer who needs a financial manager with these qualifications.

Achievements

Credited with several achievements during the course of my career. Here are three of the more noteworthy:

- Developed policies and procedures for payroll functions and information systems, resulting in a $500,000 annual savings.

- Increased revenue by 33% via the planning of pension payments and material controls.

- Consolidated EDP, payroll, and inventory control functions into one cohesive unit, which improved efficiency and omitted most chronic problems.

Employment

THE BALL BEARING COMPANY   June 1983 to Present
Title: Director of Finance

Engaged in the supervision of four (4) departments and thirty-one (31) personnel. Position requires considerable analysis with regard to domestic and international markets, and drawing conclusions about the company's production potential and the investment environ-

105

Functional Résumé

Are you highly experienced, with a diversified background? Are you concerned that an employer may not gain a full appreciation of your total capabilities if you slant your résumé one way—that is, toward a specific job or career field? The alternative to this dilemma may be to construct what is called a "functional" résumé. It presents your background as if it were a painting, and it asks the reader to see its various aspects as part of a whole. Its opening serves as a summarization of your career-to-date, and it attempts to throw light on the major experience components of your career. When you do not say what you want, however, it definitely tests the imagination of the employer as to how he could best use someone with so much to offer. That is asking a lot of someone who may not be that imaginative. Should you decide to turn yours into a functional résumé, take care to make sure that it has some sort of central theme, meaning that a general career field should be identified (e.g., business), or a major activity should be stated (e.g., management). Without either, the résumé is doomed to fail.

The Procedure

A heading like one of these is almost always first:

Introduction
Professional Profile
Career Summary
Background Synopsis

Below the heading a capsule view of your career is provided. For example:

> Presenting a 15-year background in MANAGEMENT, which is highlighted by experience with two well-known companies, one in military electronics and the other in consumer products. Have a solid knowledge of the following:

Now comes the broad brushstrokes, where major activities are mentioned first, and something is said about each. One structural example looks like this:

> ADMINISTRATION: Summarizing information pertaining to this activity is included.
>
> MARKETING: Summarizing information pertaining to this activity is included.
>
> FINANCE: Summarizing information pertaining to this activity is included.

The total summarization of your background should not be lengthy: go right to the information which you believe will interest the employer the most. Lengthy explanations are not warranted. Be reminded that your major experience components should be listed in the order of their importance.

Your skills, achievements, education, and a listing of your employers (with or without dates) follows. Since you have written about your background already, it makes little sense to repeat the same data under each employer. Beyond your job title and perhaps a brief description of the organizations(s) with which you are and were associated, any information which is placed beneath your present and former employers should be quite brief.

Conclusion

Although it is perhaps asking too much of any employer to look at a diversified background and determine how that individual would best fit into his company, for some job hunters it may nevertheless provide them with the latitude they feel they need when competing with others in the job market. Done well, it can really sell you.

Functional Résumé

When a definite job is pursued as a result of a classified ad, or because you heard about the job through the "grapevine," your cover letter, if you choose to send one along with your résumé, may give you the opportunity to be more specific. It is not a great alternative, but it will do when there is nothing else.

Internal Promotion

When vying for a position within your own company, neither a résumé in its classic sense nor a cover letter is truly appropriate. Instead, a "fact sheet" that compares your unqualified credentials with the demands of the job being pursued is far more effective. If you give your employer a regular résumé, he may think that you are currently looking for a position *outside* the company and that you only changed the first paragraph, which contains your objective, to match the opening. Do not be vague about your qualifications. Be prepared to back them up.

The Procedure

A request for an internal promotion is still a résumé; it just looks different. Here is one way of creating one.

1. At the top center of the page type your name, address, and phone number, much as you would when writing a résumé.
2. Drop down four or five spaces; then center and type "Seeking a promotion to" (or something similar), followed by the name of the job you are after. You may underline or capitalize the name of the position. If the title is too long, place a colon (:) after "to," double space down, and then type the title on that line.
3. Drop down at least three more spaces and type two headings. On the left-hand side, type the words "Requirements of Position," on the right-hand side, type the heading "My Experience." Both headings may be underlined.
4. Double space and beneath "Requirements" type the most important responsibility in that job, as a result of reviewing the actual job description itself or learning of it through talking to the person who held the position previously.

5. On the right-hand side, under "My Experience," state the experience in relation to that responsibility you have listed, making sure to keep each requirement parallel with your actual experience. In this way, the employer (or manager) who is making the decision is able to look at your two-column typewritten page and match the two without having to hunt for them.

Any achievements that might relate (money or time saved, etc.) should be included in the same section, separated perhaps by a single space.

6. Next, type the next most important function of the position, and so on.

7. These sections may also be added to the Internal Promotion Request.
   - Education
   - Work Philosophy

8. At the bottom of the page, type a line for your signature and the date you submitted the paper to the company.

Following is an outline of a request for internal promotion.

Name
Address

Seeking a promotion to _____

Requirements of position	**My experience**
State 1st requirement	Show experience
State 2nd requirement	Show experience
State 3rd requirement	Show experience
Education	
Work Philosophy	
Signature _____	**Date** _____

Imagine that the first requirement was you must have five years of experience in the development of systems to improve efficiency. On the right-hand side, exactly opposite that requirement, you might write the following:

Internal Promotion

I have a six-year background in this area, while assigned to the Department of Planning and Department of Finance. In fact, one system has saved $1.5M, and three others have become fixtures in our subsidiaries.

Pronouns like *our* and *we* should be used frequently.

Mailing the Résumé

There can be a little more to mailing a résumé than just sticking it into an envelope and dropping it into a mailbox. With regard to this otherwise meaningless activity, perhaps you may wish to use one of the techniques which follow.

An Advertisement: A résumé is an advertisement. With that in mind, it makes sense that you may send your résumé to an employer more than once when fishing for a possible job opening. The emphasis is on "fishing," as opposed to those times when you mail your résumé to an employer because of an advertisement you have seen in a newspaper or magazine. A company, for example does not advertise its products or services just one time on just one day, hoping that everyone sees it and remembers it. Neither should you.

They may send you a letter and inform you that your résumé is being kept on file and that they will contact you if anything matching your background opens in the future. You have no guarantee that it is actually kept, however. Keep sending it once every couple of weeks or once a month. Maybe one day it will hit someone's desk at just the right time.

You may want to mail your résumé to some companies more than you do some others. Develop a list of those companies you wish to contact with some frequency, which should, ideally, be no more than ten or fifteen.

A Reference Guide: When mailing your résumé, you may find it helpful to know *when* and *why* you did so — or at least have some pertinent information about that company that will make you appear knowledgeable. Should an employer call you one evening and begin chatting with you about your background, having some information at your fingertips to jog your memory about that employer could well be to your advantage. To the caller, it would certainly make you seem as if you had a great memory. This can be accomplished by creating a reference guide that is laid near your telephone, one which enables you to quickly refer to the page that contains information about the employer who is calling. A large address book works well, because companies should be recorded alphabetically. In this way, you can immediately turn to that section when you hear the employer's name.

Here are the basic aspects of a makeshift guide.

Date résumé was mailed
Name of the company
Source used to identify the company (Newspaper ad? Phone book?)
Their products or service
Job title advertised, if in a newspaper
Person to whom the résumé was sent

This approach is obviously ideal for the most thorough-minded, those who know that phone calls come from employers when one *least* expects it. Therefore, they prefer to be *prepared* rather than stumble around in their speech and come across as unprofessional. They would rather say something like this:

> "Yes, I recall sending you my résumé. I read an article about how you were planning to expand your production capabilities, and I thought my background in that area might be of benefit."

This is more desirable than waiting for the employer to carry *all* of the introductory portion of the conversation. It is simply more impressive.

Highlighting an Item: To drawn attention to something on your résumé, a broad felt-tip pen called a highlighter may be run over a few words. It can be purchased at almost any drug store, department store, or office supply shop. And of all the colors that are available, yellow is usually the most appropriate. Red is too harsh.

Mailing the Résumé

Highlighting must not be overdone; in fact, one complete line (not to be confused with a full sentence) is the maximum.

Into the Envelope: To prepare your résumé for mailing, lay it face-up on the table, the top being to your left. Lift the right-hand side and fold one-third of the paper to your left. Turn the paper over and fold the other one-third back. Place it in the envelope so that your name will be visible when the résumé is pulled out.

When your résumé is placed on someone's desk, the fold of your résumé forces your name to always show.

The Interview

The whole idea behind developing a résumé is to solicit an interview with it. The key word here is *interview*, not *job*. Unless an employer hires strictly from what he sees on paper, no résumé has ever gotten anyone a job. As stated elsewhere in this book, the most it can do is get a job hunter into the employer's office. The rest is up to him or her.

All of the information which follows does not concern the subject of résumés directly; when it does not, it explores the realities and myths that prevail about the art of seeking a job. It is just as important to understanding these factors as it is grasp the principles of effective résumé writing itself, assuming you want to generate an interview with your résumé.

Help Wanted Ads

If you are going to use them, you should be aware of these things:

- Less than 10 percent of the jobs available show up in the newspaper.

- Employers often ask for more qualifications than the position demands, so don't discount yourself because you do not meet each requirement.

- It sometimes means the employer could not, or would not, fill the job from among his own staff of people. The question is, Why?

- Most positions in the job market are filled before an employer has to resort to buying space in the help wanted section. This supports the estimate that only 10 percent of the jobs can be found in the paper.

- High-level jobs that pay well are almost never found in the "help wanted" section.

- Blind ads are extremely dangerous for the job hunter who is employed, despite all of the so-called safeguards. There is no guarantee, for example, that your résumé will be screened from the flood of others which may be going directly to your boss.

Here are some things you should or should not do.

- Never restrict you attention to the ads which seem to apply to your experience only. For example, am employer who is looking for a bookkeeper might even need an accountant, a secretary, etc.

- Review help wanted ads in the back issues of newspapers to see hiring trends of an employer. These are available, on microfilm, at the library.

- When an ad says you can make thousands of dollars per week, and it reads like it could fit almost anyone, don't send your résumé.

Headhunters

They are not all the same. Executive Search Consultants specialize in certain fields and are hired by companies to find a particular executive-type, and they receive—from the employer—30 percent to 35 percent of the executive's first year's salary. They recruit people *away* from other employers rather than find jobs *for* an individual. They write the résumé, which the executive never sees. There are other groups which say they are Executive Search Consultants, but they require money from the individual—up front. It often turns out that you, the job seeker, get nothing more than many copies of a very expensive résumé, which they never use to promote you.

Employment agents usually expect to be given a résumé. You owe him a commission fee if you accept a job that isn't fee paid, or if an employer hires you for a position *other than* the one for which the agent referred you. Further, you must tell him which employers you have contacted before seeing him, for he is forbidden to duplicate your efforts. He is rarely an expert in the job market, and he will usually work harder for you when you are employed than when you are not.

To find an agency with a good reputation, try phoning various personnel departments of reputable companies and ask for referrals. You might say, "I'm considering looking for employment, and I've decided I want a professional to present my background to employers. Since I care too much about my career to just blindly pick one out of the Yellow Pages, and since you deal with them regularly, I wonder if you would know of any good consultants that I might call." If possible, try to talk to the personnel manager. She may be impressed with your approach and might want to know more about you for an opening in her company.

No headhunter can convince an employer to hire you; that's your job.

Books on Job Hunting

None can be all-knowing or all wrong, but they should be read. In fact, you should become a student of job hunting. Not only is it necessary for you to know as much about job hunting as you possibly can, in order to protect yourself, but you should also gain a deeper appreciation of how important it is to continuously collect information for your future résumé rather than wait until the last minute.

Job Search Principles

- Chase a career, not security.

- Your employer's direct competitors are usually willing to pay more money than anyone else to get you, because they do not have to train you.

- Construct a general plan and be true to it. Use whatever approach works best for you, or that with which you feel most comfortable. If that means stealing bits and pieces from different job getting formulas, then do it.

- Develop a habit of asking other people how they got *their* jobs. You may learn about a new technique.

- Before you decide to change careers, interview as many people as you can in the other field to be sure that you are not making a career move that you will later regret.

- Do not look for a job by phone.

- The best time to look for another job is when you are already employed, for there is no substitute for dealing from a position of strength. Employers are leery of those who are out of work and looking for a job.

- Cover letters need only accompany your résumé when you have something extra special to say.

- Timing plays a great role in getting an interview from a résumé. The same person may look at the same résumé on two different days and have totally different reactions: one positive and one negative.

- Monday is not a good interview day. It is usually the busiest, phone calls are more likely to interrupt the interview, and you compete with more applicants on that day. But if Monday is all you can get, take it.

- Some mannerisms to some employers are irritating (e.g., foot wiggling, finger tapping, etc.), and the less you have the better off you will be. If you have one that has gotten out of hand, try to rid yourself of it.

Before and During the Interview

Reading articles about an employer prior to an interview can make you appear quite knowledgeable, if you use any of the information in an off-the-cuff manner during the conversation. It is flattering to the employer. If such articles do exist, they can be found in back issues of magazines and newspapers at your main library. People who are now, or have been, employed by a company with which you have an interview can tell you far more than you will receive from most sources.

Always confirm the interview the day before. Take an extra copy of your résumé to the interview with you, because things get lost. Also take along a list of your references, and a notepad and pen.

Contacted by Phone: When contacted by phone, you can be assured of one thing: The employer has seen something in your résumé that he likes. Your task is to find out what it is by asking a direct question as soon as you possibly can. You might ask, "What specific aspect of my background interested you the most?" If you are told, then promote that and nothing more. In other words, do not sell all of your other skills or experience. Also push for the interview, so that you can sell it in person rather than allow him to interview you over the phone. Nothing replaces the handshake and actual visual contact.

There is another way to accomplish the same thing, and it can be done by asking this question early in the conversation: "What are the requirements of the job for which I am presently being considered?" When he responds, you know what is *wanted;* next, you will have to fill in the blanks by relating your background to as many of them as possible.

Bad Reference: If you feel a former employer may be giving you a bad reference, you are within your legal right to review what has been written about you in your personnel file. Further, you may challenge it when you feel it is an unfair representation.

Salary Discussion: Allowing the employer to talk money with you before he extends a firm offer of employment places you at a disadvantage. However, if an employer presents you with a low and high salary range as a starting point, pick the highest. It is easier to negotiate downward than it is upwards. When an employer refuses to raise his salary offer, you are usually forced to accept or decline. When a salary is agreed upon, ask that the agreement be formalized by having everything put in writing. What you don't want is to tell your present boss that you are quitting, only to find out later that something drastic has happened at your new company, leaving your new job in shambles. Now, you don't have either job.

Don't envision an offer exceeding your present salary by more than 20 percent. Fringe benefits have nothing to do with your salary, and don't be persuaded by the hiring employer that they do.

Interview Questions: To prepare you for the unexpected, here are some questions you may be asked during an interview.

1. What do you think of your present boss?
2. What is your greatest weakness?
3. Are you most like your father or mother? Why?
4. Why do you want to leave your present employer?
5. Why did you leave your other employers?
6. What do you enjoy the least about your work?
7. What are your short-range goals?
8. What are your long-range goals?
9. What is your own personal definition of success?
10. What was the last book you read?
11. What type of book do you most enjoy? Why?
12. What type of movies do you like? Why?
13. What is your favorite TV show? Why?
14. To which magazines do you subscribe? Why?
15. Which individual in the world do you most admire? Why?
16. What person has had the most influence in your life? Why?
17. If you could start all over again, what would you change?
18. If you could step into any type of job, what would it be?

Some questions *you* may want to ask, the answers of which may tell you a great deal about the job, the company, or the person for whom you will be working.

1. How many have held this job over the last five years?
2. Is there much turnover in this position?
3. Is this job new, or has it been around for a while?
4. Why isn't someone from within the organization being promoted to this position?
5. If this job suddenly failed to exist, what repercussions would that have in the company? (Tells you how important it is.)
6. How many people will I be reporting to?

The Interview

7. On your organizational chart, can you show me exactly where this position stands?
8. What's the next natural step after this position? Who holds that position? How long has he been there?
9. Concerning the duties of this position, what are the top three in the order of their importance?
10. For the next person who holds this position, what do you consider the most difficult problem he or she will encounter?
11. Among the people who have held this job so far, what has been their biggest gripe about it?
12. Do you have in mind any specific results you want to see produced by someone who holds this position? Is there one thing you want to see done above all the others?
13. Excluding their own personal lives outside the company, can you give me a synopsis of each person I would be working (or dealing) with?
14. What is the most significant accomplishment of the person I would be replacing?
15. What is your own management philosophy?
16. If you could change one thing about this company to make it better, what would that be?
17. What do you like the most about working here?
18. Which is the most pressing problem facing your management staff right now?
19. Have you been looking for someone for this position for a long time?

Letters

In this section you will find samples of letters which you may wish to use to accompany your résumé, or to communicate with your future or present employer. None are obligatory; but in the case of accepting a job offer and resigning from your present company, they may prove to be quite necessary for your own self-protection.

The Cover Letter

The term probably originated when someone tried to cover up a poorly written résumé with a better-written letter. It is sometimes called a "covering" letter, but we choose to look at it as a two-word noun; hence, the *ing* is dropped.

Under no circumstances should you believe it can cover up a bad résumé. If you have a bad résumé, the best cover letter in the world won't save it. On the other hand, if you have a good résumé, very often a cover letter is unnecessary, becoming a gross misuse of paper and saying nothing more than what is already presented in the résumé itself. A cover letter cannot advertise you; only your résumé will. Cover letters get lost. It is not at all unusual for a cover letter to become separated from the résumés they accompany (this is because they should not be stapled).

The typewriter or word processor used to produce your résumé should be used to construct your cover letter as well. Nothing can look worse than matching up a professionally prepared résumé in one type-style with a cover letter that displays a completely different kind. Further, if someone types your résumé for you, you will have to keep going back there each time you want a cover letter prepared.

When you write the cover letter, begin with a one- or two-sentence paragraph that explains why the résumé is being sent. An exception to this occurs when answering a help-wanted ad. The employer knows why you are sending it. Follow the first paragraph with another that promotes your qualifications. End the letter with a one- or two-sentence paragraph that expresses thanks to the reader for his consideration.

Three Examples: This first example is from a new graduate, who begins the letter with a bit of flattery. In the second paragraph he tells the company that he would like to get involved in what they are doing (which means he knows something about the company), and he throws in a couple of personal characteristics about himself. The last paragraph consists of a single question.

> Dear Sir:
>
> Since your organization has an excellent reputation in the area of transportation, I am enclosing my résumé for your review.
>
> I will be receiving my B.S. in transportation in June of this year, and I wish to become a member of a company like yours, which is engaged in the design, development, and marketing of high speed transit systems. Filled with ideas and eager to establish a career in this field, I want to be a part of a superior design team.
>
> Should you find my credentials of interest to you, may we get together soon and discuss how I can add to your company's growing success?

In this next example, notice that the job hunter mentions his experience in a major field. In the second paragraph he becomes more specific. The last paragraph is comprised of two brief sentences.

> Dear Sir:
>
> I have ten years of experience in the safety field, which is supported by a solid formal education in this area as well, and I am exploring the possibility of changing employers.
>
> I have an expertise in the design of safety devices for high-volume production, and I have also served as a safety educator within the plant and as a volunteer within the community. My goal is to assume a position that will provide a new, stimulating challenge.
>
> My résumé is enclosed. Your consideration is greatly appreciated.

Letters

Finally, here is an example of a cover letter where the job hunter takes an aggressive approach in the last paragraph.

> Should your company need a sales professional who has an excellent background in promoting tinker toys to tired executives, I offer my résumé for your review.
>
> I have been the top sales producer for my company over the last five years, and I have developed new territories into excellent profit areas.
>
> I would enjoy talking with you. I will call you on the morning of the 15th to ascertain your interest.

Ideally, a cover letter is short and to the point. It is not an equivalent to a short story. Nor should it contain excuses — that is, attempt to explain away something which can be found on the résumé. If that is the case, that information should not be on your résumé.

Stationery: If your résumé is printed or copied on a special kind of paper, and you have intentions of sending cover letters along with it, then getting blank sheets of that paper is essential. Unmatched colors and textures of paper can be just as unprofessional as having unmatched typestyles. Consistency must be maintained; otherwise it has a jarring effect on the reader. But should you go so far as to have your name and address printed on the blank sheets? Not necessarily. While a résumé is indeed an advertisement, "personalized" stationary can be a bit showy for some job hunters and actually serve to harm one's chances. The general rule of thumb is this: If you are in a position (high-level or not) where personalized stationary is second nature, then by all means continue the trend. But there is no need to do so otherwise.

Getting Names: When mailing a cover letter with your résumé and you need the name of someone to direct it to, the phone is a handy way of accomplishing that end. Merely call into a company department and, using some pretext and a fictitious name of your own choosing, attempt to determine the name of the manager. Consider, too, that the manager himself might answer; therefore, you will need an especially good reason why you want that name. Writing out what you want to say in advance helps a great deal.

Trade directories, which are found at your central library, offer a source for names within companies, but they can quickly grow out of date because of the natural movement of people from company to company. One way around this is by using the phone again and asking the person on the other end of the line if Mr. So and So is still the manager of a particular department. If he isn't, ask for the name of his replacement. Sometimes they'll even tell you where the other manager went, which becomes another possible lead.

The Memo

There is an alternative to the typewritten cover letter, something you can do very quickly and which has a personal touch, something which the employer almost always reads. It is called the memo.

The use of notes is widespread, and people feel comfortable with this time-saving approach. The fact that something can be written without going though all the formalities of having it typed certainly makes it convenient. Also, the memo comes with these advantages:

- No date, address, salutation, or *Yours truly* is needed.

- Handwritten information is more personal and is far more likely to be read.

What is being suggested here is that you may use a handwritten memo instead of a cover letter and attach it to your résumé. In fact, unlike the cover letter, you may actually staple it to the résumé itself. The memo approach does not adapt itself well to all fields, or even to all individuals.

Here are the steps you may wish to take, assuming this approach interests you. If you have your résumé printed on special paper, acquire about ten extra sheets of that paper. More if you like. Have the paper cut in the middle both ways, which will give you 40 "memo sheets" of equal size. When writing a note to an employer, never date it and never write "Dear Sir." If you know the recipient's name, simply write Mr. or Ms., the individual's last name, and then add a colon (:) or a dash (−). Otherwise simply write your note without a salutation. Compose a very short note, expressing your interest in the organization or describing your credentials. If your handwriting is bad, try printing the letters — or let someone in your family do it for you. The personal touch is very important. Do not write "Sincerely" or anything similar. Merely sign your name. Staple the note to the upper left corner of your résumé. Paper clips get lost, along with the memo. Should you decide to have your name printed on the memos, the printer will have to do that before they are cut. In that event, have your name placed at either the upper-left or the bottom right-hand corner. No address or phone number is required; that is already on your résumé. Blank paper, however, is perfectly acceptable — and less expensive.

Do not send a memo to a prospective employer with one of those trite phrases at the top which says something like "From the Desk of. . . ."

The Broadcast Letter

Earlier, in the section regarding the development of a résumé, this concept could have been introduced as an alternative. Because it is a letter in nature, however, and because it is a technique that is often impractical for many people to use, an explanation about it has been delayed until now. Like any letter, it is directed to one person. A personnel manager should not be its recipient; rather, it is sent to managers of departments, divisions, or companies. It is used in place of the traditional résumé when contacting employers. One page in length, it is designed to look like a personal letter, although it is really an abbreviated résumé. When sent to a manager in pursuit of a specific job or area of employment, it can be a powerful vehicle that will gain an interview for you. Much of this rides on the fact that it is originally prepared — that is, it is not printed or copied — addressed to a specific individual, and personally signed, as a letter should be. Statistically, a broadcast letter is far more prone to be read than the average résumé because of the personal touch that attends it. This personalized, abbreviated résumé-in-disguise is a concentrated sales pitch that provides the reader with a good synopsis of your background, objective, skills, accomplishments, and education. It also permits you to keep the names of your present and former employers secret until you desire to divulge them, thereby creating some measure of protection.

The broadcast letter only eliminates the résumé at the outset, however. An employer who becomes interested in your background, as a result of the broadcast letter, will want to see a more in-depth résumé during the interview, possibly even before. Consequently, you wind up doing double work to achieve the same end.

You should not send another broadcast letter to the same person if the first one fails to open any doors. To send it again to the same individual a couple of weeks later is not much different than sending a copy of the same letter to the same friend who you wrote to last week. It must be tailored to the employer who is receiving it, causing some research to be done and the editing of that information down to one or two lines, where it may be inserted into the broadcast letter. This, too, costs you time and effort. Whether it is worth it or not depends upon the level of job you are seeking and a host of other factors.

It must be originally produced each time — a drawback when you are considering mailing it to a great many employers. Pre-printing, therefore, is out of the question. If you have access to data processing equipment that has letter-quality printing, however, recreating the letter is hardly a problem. Here is just one example of a broadcast letter:

Dear Mr. Hiring:

I have long respected your company's reputation in the field of publishing, and I am a supporter of your advertising philosophy as outlined in the January edition of Forbes Magazine.

For myself, I have acquired more than *five years of experience in the field of advertising sales, and I've generated more than $3.6M in revenue during this period.* My employers have included a major metropolitan newspaper, a national magazine, and a widely distributed, prestigious trade publication. Among my peers, I am considered to be highly knowledgeable in my field.

Currently I desire to apply this experience toward a position in *sales management,* specifically with a quality publishing house such as yours. I can do the following:

- — develop new promotional concepts that produce profits for both customer and employer
- — significantly widen the base of repeat customers.
- — create visual aids for major presentations.
- — anticipate and solve problems before they develop.

132

My background includes communication with a wide range of customers, national and local, and I have devised unique ways to promote their products or services, which has earned for me an excellent reputation as a "creative sales promoter." I am experienced in the areas of developing ad layouts, and have become a full-time student concerning the artistic end of the business to better serve clients.

I acquired an M.B.A. from the University of Kentucky and a B.B.A. from Ohio State University. Moreover, I keep up-to-date in my profession by attending numerous seminars in management and advertising.

If you should desire to discuss my potential worth to your organization, you may reach me at (312) 444-1212 after 6 P.M. during the week.

A complete résumé is available upon your request.

Sincerely,

Outtava Jopp

Letter on Behalf

On the chance that you know someone of influence, preferably someone like a department manager or an owner of a company, you may be able to get him or her to write to a specific company on your behalf. This is a highly questionable option, but one which must be included.

Using his own stationery, of course, and possibly even given an outline of what you would like to see in the letter, here is an example:

Dear Mr. Smith:

As the vice-president of manufacturing for the XYZ Company, I would like to take this opportunity to tell you about someone who I think would make a great addition to your own company.

His name is ____(your name)____, and I regret that we cannot make room for him in our organization. He is a solid professional in the field of finance, and he has saved his employers about $2.3M over a three-year period. He is quite adept at developing long-range investment programs.

Because of his company's decision to relocate back to Maine, he will soon be facing unemployment. He wishes to remain here in this city.

I have informed him that I will be contacting several prestigious companies on his behalf. I suspect you will be getting a phone call from him later this week.

Your consideration is greatly appreciated.

Admittedly, most job seekers will not have the luxury of having such an influential friend going to bat for them. And if they did, there is indeed a serious question about whether or not they would want to test the friendship in this manner.

Acceptance Letter

When your interview with a company results in their making you an offer of a job, a letter of acceptance is often due from you. That job offer may be extended at the end of the interview, whereupon, as stated previously, you should get them to put the details down on paper and sign it. On the other hand, the job offer may come over the phone, or through the mail, sometime after the interview.

Especially in the case when the job offer is delayed, the points you bring out in the acceptance letter can be important. This letter should be typed via a word processing program that *dates* entries. This, too, is another reason why it is advantageous to have your own computer disk which contains your résumé on it. You can put your acceptance letter on that disk, and the date and time it was typed will automatically be attached to it. It is like having it notarized, only your future employer does not know it.

Here are some of the major points you may wish to include in your acceptance letter—just in case your future boss has already forgotten the finer details.

- Title of the position being offered to you
- Name of the division/department
- Name of your new boss
- Date you expect to start work
- Salary (weekly, monthly, yearly?)
- Bonuses (based on what?)
- Hospitalization

- Vacation
- Other fringe benefits (e.g., car, etc.)

An example of an acceptance letter is as follows:

> Dear Mr. _____:
>
> This letter is to inform you that I have agreed to accept your offer of employment and that I will be starting work as a program coordinator within the creative department of the Dumb Division on July 4, 1999. I look forward to being a part of Felix Fing's team.
>
> Also, I agree to the following terms of employment as set forth in your letter, dated June 15, 1999. These terms include a $500,000 annual salary, paid bi-weekly at $19,230.77, a four-month vacation; a full-coverage hospitalization and dental program.
>
> I'm sure I will find it a pleasure working for a company that is recognized for its high quality product line.
>
> Sincerely,
>
> Happy Asalark

Declining an Offer

Declining an offer is a nice position in which to be. On the other hand, it is no time to be blunt. You are still dealing with human beings, and they are prone to go from employer to employer over the course of their careers. Perhaps your paths may cross again, and your lack of good will might well be remembered at a time and place where you least expect it—not that you would ever know it, of course.

Declining the offer comes in the second paragraph, while at the same time praising the employer in some way. Here is an example:

> Dear Mr. Shine:
>
> I would like to take this opportunity to thank you for your generous offer of employment, which I received on August 2, 1987. The position of Company Flunky certainly is of interest to me, and I greatly enjoyed visiting your facilities on July 23, 1987.

However, I have received several offers from other organizations as well, and—after much deliberation—I have decided to accept an offer presented to me by another company. Of the offers I have received, I must be honest with you and inform you that the quality of your company and that of my future employer made that decision highly difficult. I am convinced that my future within your firm would have been just as bright.

In the years to come, I am sure that we will cross paths again, and no doubt my decision will be completely different. Again, I thank you for the career opportunity you offered.

Sincerely,

Ben Goodtanoya

A Resignation Letter

Basically you only want to tell your present boss when you will be leaving, that you will help train anyone else in the meantime, and somehow convey the thought that you feel your experience under his direction was beneficial, despite how you really feel. An example:

Dear _____:

This letter is to inform you that I will be resigning my position at Ajax Chemical, effective October 16, 1995, for I have accepted employment with another company. Prior to my leaving, of course, I will be happy to train another individual to assume my duties, if you like.

I feel that my association with your department has been a fortunate occurrence in my career. Thank you for the opportunity and the trust you have shown me.

If your boss gets mad because you are leaving, and he tells you to leave now, then leave. At least you tried. You did the honorable thing. Be sure your letter of acceptance has been mailed to your new employer.

The Business Card

This is not the kind of business card that you are normally used to seeing. It is, in fact, a mini-résumé which is attached to any résumé you send through the mail. When an employer does not have any current interest in hiring someone with your background, it is quite unlikely that your résumé will be saved for a later date when he might indeed need you. But there is a far better chance that a business card-size résumé will be kept, because it is easier to store. It is also the kind of résumé which you can easily carry with you.

The Contents: Even though both sides of the card are used, the fact that it is small—measuring only 2″ × 3½″—precludes any idea of cramming it full of information.

On the front side of the card is included the following:
1. Your name
2. A single line about your experience, placed just below your name
3. Your address and phone number, which occupy both bottom corners.

Here is an example:

John A. Doe
Fifteen years in Administrative Management
(see back of this card)

2524 Agnes Road
Brookhaven, N.Y. 21079   (212) 688-9292

You may make the card as conservative or as bold as you wish, but it should be in harmony with the nature of your career. A job hunter who is looking for a position to utilize his or her artistic abilities would probably not want to be as plain as the example you see above.

On the back side of the card is placed all of the pertinent information about your background. To include as much as possible in such a short space—yet leaving enough whitespace to prevent a crowded look—the editing skills which you have acquired will be put to their greatest test. Possible categories include your major experience components, skills, achievements, education, job titles, etc.

Here is an example of how one might look.

```
Purchasing, Finance, Personnel,
Data Processing, Payroll, Sys-
tems, & Manual Development.


Skills include problem-solving,
employee motivation, writing
reports, planning/scheduling,
and cost control.


Dramatically improved systems
efficiency with present em-
ployer. Saved former company
$25,000.


M.B.A./Finance major
B.B.A./Accounting
```

Using such business cards to attach to your résumé, or to give to someone whenever the time seems appropriate, is really an option that should only be adopted by those who are more keenly motivated about finding a better job.

Index

Acceptance letter 134–35
Achievement(s) 36–40; editing 66–68; headings, types of 37; methods of recording 37–40
Activities 42–43; new graduate 43
Address 3–4
Awards 44

Book reading 24
Broadcast letter 131–33
Business card 136–38

Career changer: defined 1; describing past employment 35; employing "preface" 63; résumé layout 71–72
Career fields: list of 5–6
Career objective see Opening paragraph
Children see Personal data
Class projects 33–35
College courses 22
College expenses 19–20
Company course 22
Co-op experience 32–33
Correspondence course 22
Cover letter 127–29

Date of birth see Personal data
Date of employment see Employment dates
Dean's List 19
Declining job offer 135–36
Design: bullets, asterisks, etc. 79; conclusion 80; importance of 72; photo-graph 79–80; typing 73–77; whitespace 77–78

Editing 47–52
Education: book reading 24; college degrees 15–16; college expenses 19–20; company course 22; correspondence course 22; dean's list 19; editing 57–59; education intentions 25; grade point average 18–19; headings, types of 14; high school 23–24; honors 18; impact on employers 15–16; individual courses 20; military 22–23; no degree 20–21; order of importance 14–15; scholarship 17–18; seminar 21–22
Employer(s), name of 26
Employment: career changer 35; dates 65; describing past employers 8–9; editing 59–66; heading, types of 25–26; job description 28–31; job title 26–27; knowledge gained 31; military background 35–36; name of employer 26; new graduate 31–35; reason for leaving 31; salary (present) 27; summarized 6–8; work environment 27–28
Experience see Employment

First paragraph see Opening paragraph
Functional résumé 107

Grade point average 18–19
Graduate (new): activities 42–43; class

Index

project 33–35; college expenses 19–
20; co-op experience 32–33; defined
1; summer job 31–32

Headings: achievements 37; education
14; employment 25–26; employment
preface 62; functional résumé 107;
job objective 4; opening paragraph 4;
personal profile 10; skills 10
Health *see* Personal data
Height *see* Personal data
High school 23–24
Hobbies 42
Honors 18
How others see you 13–14

Interests 42
Interview: bad reference 123; contacted
by phone 123; headhunters 20–27;
job hunting books 121; job search
principles 121–22; talking salary 123–
124

Job changer *see* Career changer
Job description 28–31
Job environment 27–28
Job hunters, defined 1–2
Job objective *see* Opening paragraph
Job preferences 9–10
Job title(s) 26–27

Knowledge gained: employment 31;
method of determining 6–8

Layout 71–72
Length 83–84
Letter: broadcast 131–33; cover 127–30;
declining job offer 135–36; getting
names 129–30; job acceptance 134–
35; letter on behalf 133–34; "memo"
130–31; resignation letter 136; stationery 129

Major (degree) 16–17
Marital status *see* Personal data
Memberships 42
"Memo" *see* Letter "memo"
Military: background 45; dischargee de-
fined 2; education 22–23; experience
35–36; rank 36
Minor (degree) 17

Name, personal 3

Objective *see* Opening paragraph
Opening paragraph: choosing major
career field 5–6; description of employers 8–9; describing past employers 8–9; editing 52–55; experience summarized 6–8; headings,
types of 4; job objective, indefinite 5–
6; job objective, specific 5; job
preferences 9–10; knowledge gained
6–8; opening words 5; statement of
experience 6–8

Part-time job 31
Personal data 44
Personal profile 10–14; headings, types
of 10; perception 13–14; skills 10–12;
talents (innate) 12–13
Philosophy 41
Phone number 3–4
Printing 84–86
Proofreading 81
Publications 45

Quotes *see* Testimonials

Rank 36
Reason for leaving 31
References 46

Index

Resignation letter 136
Résumés, sample 87–105

Talents 12–13, 56, 57
Telephone number 4
Testimonials 40–41
Title(s), job 26–27; military rank 36

Salary: present 27; requirement
  46
Skills 10–12
Summer job 31–32

Weight *see* Personal data
Work: description 28–31; environment
  27–28; philosophy 41

141